Jump Start Your School!

Fifty Short-term Objectives to Improve Performance

by

SEAN CAIN

Copyright © 2009 Sean Cain
All rights reserved

ISBN: 1-4392-3769-7
EAN13: 9781439237694

Visit www.booksurge.com to order additional copies.

DEDICATION

For Lesa

Table of Contents

Introduction. . . . . Page 1

Chapter 1: Getting Started . . . . Page 5

Chapter 2: Discipline and Behavior . . . . Page 11

Chapter 3: Instructional Rigor and Relevance. . . . . Page 41

Chapter 4: Literacy . . . . Page 99

Chapter 5: Grades and Grading . . . . Page 115

Chapter 6: Student Engagement . . . . Page 147

Chapter 7: Special Needs . . . . Page 153

Chapter 8: Communication Skills. . . . . Page 163

Chapter 9: School Clubs, Co-curricular Activities, . . Page 181
            Extracurricular Activities, and
            Community Service

Chapter 10: Technology . . . . Page 195

Chapter 11: Graduation and Beyond. . . . . Page 201

Chapter 12: Rubrics . . . . Page 225

Chapter 13: Conclusion . . . . Page 227

Glossary of Names and Terms: . . . . Page 229

Works Cited. . . . . Page 237

Jump Start Your School!

Introduction

I have friends, friends that are principals at schools all across the country. These friends are unique, unique in the sense that they went to lead schools that no one thought had any realistic chance of improving, much less improving rapidly. Yet, over and over again, these principals have proven the naysayers wrong. Their results have often bordered on miraculous, especially when compared to their peer principals who are leading similar schools.

So how do they do it? Why are these principals and their schools experiencing unprecedented success? What are their secrets? What do these principals, regardless of the size, wealth, grade level, and setting of their school do different than everyone else?

When you talk to these principals and their staff, and then observe their work, it quickly becomes apparent that they adhere to some fundamental beliefs:

The first fundamental belief is that movement requires friction. Constant progress makes some people uncomfortable and that is okay. Adults get paid to work and adapt. It is their job to deal with their discomfort and keep moving forward. When the choice boils down to student success or adult comfort, these principals always opt for the students.

The second fundamental belief is that long-term gains are best achieved by accomplishing strands of short-term goals and objectives. These principals are experts at articulating, in concrete language, exactly what they expect in both student and adult performance in very short-term increments. As their campuses begin to meet short-term achievement targets consistently, dramatic annual improvement becomes almost automatic. This process is similar to what a prudent driver does when she is planning a trip to an unfamiliar location. First, she selects her destination. Then she gets her map and selects a route. On the route, she notes waypoints and estimates the time it will take to reach those waypoints. As she passes waypoints on her route, she is confident that she will reach her destination. If she misses a waypoint, she will consult her map and decide if she should return to the last waypoint or re-adjust her route. She continues to track her progress until she arrives safely at her destination. Like the driver in the example, these principals are not surprised by the performance targets that their campuses meet. These principals understand that exceptional performance is the result of a well executed plan.

The third fundamental belief is that campus culture and climate is critical - not culture and climate as matter of luck and chance, but culture and climate by design. To make this actionable, these principals subscribe to the following definition of culture and climate:

Culture: The things that are done on a campus and the way those things are done.

Climate: Climate is the positive or negative impact that that the culture of a campus has on students.

For school leaders operating under this definition, managing climate and culture is about doing more of the things that have a positive impact on students and instruction and eliminating the things that do not. By rigorously adhering to this belief and course of action, a campus can quickly become more student-centric and academically pro-active.

Understand that jump starting your school is not about firing staff or becoming a dictator. It is about being completely focused on student performance. Though this focus on student performance in the short run can often be unpopular, in the long run it has been observed that as student performance improves, so do the attitudes of adults. There is nothing more motivating and enriching to educators than student success.

The purpose of this is book twofold. First, it provides the author with an opportunity to share a number of powerful practices observed during a career as a teacher, principal, central office administrator, and the lead school improvement specialist for the State of Texas. Just as exceptional teaching is a combination of science and art, this book touches on both the research base that drives best practice and the results of artful, campus-based implementation of sound instructional strategies.

The second reason for writing this book is to give motivated school leaders and their staff fifty ways to jump start their school. This book will assist school and teacher leaders in creating renewed excitement and driving dramatic gains in student performance. The following fifty short-term objectives address almost all facets of a campus and its instructional program. Using them will build a solid foundation for achieving ambitious and aggressive annual goals. Simply select the ones that, based on your assessment of your campus, you believe will make the biggest positive impact, and go to work. Your staff will surprise you, your students will amaze you, and the community will thank you. Good luck!

Chapter 1: Getting Started

Getting started is easy, and the sooner a campus aggressively begins to use a selection of these jump-start objectives, the better. By starting today, a school leader can begin the process of transforming his or her school into a more nimble and proactive entity, as opposed to the mired, reactionary organization that many schools have become.

One will notice while considering the jump-start ideas presented in this book that the objective statements are both short and concrete. This is by design. The objectives and expectations for a campus must be clear. The more ambiguous the language, the less chance the staff have of achieving the school's objectives. This is especially true as the size of the staff increases. Like the "telephone game" that children play, even a short message repeated from one person to the next becomes more and more distorted. By keeping the objective concrete, precise, and measurable, message distortion is greatly limited.

One should also notice that the focus is always on results, not process. It is not because processes are not important, they are. Process is the means to achieving the objective. But the process is not an end in itself. If a campus is not achieving expected results, then the processes in use must be adapted or replaced. To put this process-versus-results concept into context, consider the following example. A jump-start objective would not be to train the entire staff in literacy coaching strategies (a worthy process). The jump-start objective would be to increase students' reading performance. The literacy coaching training is the process, the student reading performance is the result. Always focus on the results.

Some educators find this focus on results to be a difficult concept to come to grips with; they want to believe their initiatives and work should be independent of performance. This is not the case. In fact, in this new era of accountability, if the results are not to standard, the work is immediately in question. Fortunately, as mentioned in the introduction, dramatic improvement and excellent results can be achieved at any campus.

As a campus becomes more comfortable with the concept of using short-term objectives, and has experienced success using a selection of the jump-start ideas in this book, it is recommended that objectives that are unique to the campus then be developed. At the end of this chapter, there is a development template that campuses can use.

Once a jump-start objective has been chosen, an important next step is to select a measurement cycle. The rule of thumb is to select a measurement cycle that is long enough to observe a change and short enough to provide ample opportunity to make critical adjustments, if necessary. With that in mind, measurement cycles between the lengths of two weeks to a semester are recommended, with three to nine weeks being most common. Annual measurement cycles are generally not appropriate. The reason for this is by the time annual data has been collected and analyzed the die has already been cast. The odds of meeting the desired target are diminished with no regular opportunities to assess if the plan is working, and make necessary adjustments. In terms of jump starting a school, the rule is to "go short, to achieve big."

After the measurement cycle has been determined, the objective target needs to be selected. A common question is should a "realistic" target or an "ambitious" target be selected? Conventional wisdom suggests that the selected target should be one that fits the personality of the school leader and the staff. Conventional wisdom is proving to be wrong in this case. The correct answer to the question of target selection comes from the coaching community. In roles as a school leader and a school improvement specialist, the author has met with numerous successful coaches. During discussions and interviews concerning their goals for their teams, the responses from these coaches has been surprisingly consistent. Their goal, regardless of the team or the sport, is to compete for and win the championship. Then, based on their personnel, environmental factors, performance data, and results, they adjust their processes, procedures, and practices to put their teams in the best possible position to win.

A great school leader does the same thing. A great leader has ambitious goals; he or she wants all of the students to be successful and competitive, now. That is the goal and everyone knows it, staff, students, and the community. Then, the leader and the staff work and adjust everyday to achieve the goal. As such, when selecting the target for a given jump-start objective, the recommendation is to be ambitious and audacious. Set the bar high. Dare to achieve greatness.

For school leaders that want to create their own jump-start objectives the following instructions and development template should prove to be useful.

Developing Jump-start Objectives:

1) For each significant campus goal, select or develop one to three jump-start objectives.
   a. First Key: Develop an objective, that if it is on target, one can be confident that a number of other things are moving in the right direction.
      i. Example 1: If Advance Placement (AP) course enrollment is up, then pre-AP course enrollment most likely is up (if pre-AP courses are a prerequisite for AP courses).
      ii. Example 2: If the number of students passing all sections of the state competency exam is up, then the number of students passing each individual section must be up.
   b. Second Key: Identify the appropriate benchmark measure.
      i. The benchmark measure is the most recent relevant result. Common benchmarks are the results from the last year, last semester, or the last grading period.

    ii. The benchmark makes it possible to gauge progress and better determine which actions and initiatives appear to hold the most promise.

    iii. If an appropriate benchmark is not readily available, enter N/A (not applicable), and use the results from the first measurement cycle.

  c. Third Key: Use the shortest reasonable measurement cycle.

    i. With short-term measurement cycles, whether performance is good or bad, appropriate adjustments can be made to maximum results.

    ii. The shorter the time window, the easier it is to maintain a sense of urgency.

    iii. By meeting the appropriate short-term objectives, achieving the long-term goal becomes almost automatic.

2) View jump-start objectives as always in draft stage. At the end of each year, re-visit the objectives that were used to determine if there is a more appropriate measure for the goal.

  a. Example: After studying their objectives for a couple of years, one school realized that the leading indicator for a reduction in the number of fights on campus was a significant reduction in the number of campus tardy and dress code violations.

3) Finally, if an appropriate student measure cannot be identified, look for an indicator that tracks a change in adult practice.

   a. Example: Teachers instructing at higher levels of rigor is considered by many to be a significant step towards students becoming critical problem solvers.

Jump-start Objective Development Template:

Think of the jump-start objective template as an executive summary. It does not explain the entire process; it just communicates the desired effect in concrete, measurable terms.

- **Objective:** _____
  Our school will (increase / decrease)

- **Target:** _____

- **Benchmark:** _____

- **Measurement Cycle:** _____

Chapter 2: Discipline and Behavior

When it comes to improving a school rapidly, student discipline and behavior is either the most critical component needing to be addressed or simply a maintenance issue. How does one assess its importance for a particular campus? It is easy. If the campus more resembles a zoo than a place of engaged learning, then the first objective must be to regain control of the campus and provide an environment conducive to instruction. There is no question that chronic behavior problems on a campus grind meaningful instruction to a halt.

If student discipline is such that teaching and learning can occur, then this category of jump-start objectives becomes more of a monitoring issue. Discipline should remain an area that a campus strives to improve because good student behavior enhances academic performance, though it is not a primary focus everyday.

Do know that except in the most extreme cases, student discipline is best addressed through an overall focus on providing quality and engaging instruction for all students and the consistent daily modeling of student behavioral expectations by all staff. For school leaders that are seeking additional support in the area of student discipline and behavior, Lead Your School provides schools and districts with training and specific programs that increase both staff competency and confidence in the areas of improved instruction, student engagement strategies, and discipline continuum development. Further information can be found at www.leadyourschool.com.

Each of the following seven jump-start objectives presented in this chapter have made a positive impact on numerous campuses. When deciding which objectives to implement, select the ones that best address the most critical discipline and behavior issues currently impacting the school.

Objective #1:   Discipline and Behavior

Our school will decrease the number of office referrals.

Objective Target:	At least a 10 percent decrease in referrals should be selected.
Measurement Cycle:	Select three weeks, six weeks, or nine weeks.
Campus Levels:	This objective is appropriate for campuses serving any grade level.
Why:	The positive adult practices and school systems that reduce discipline referrals also support increased student performance (McClure & Spector, 1997).
Power:	As student behavior improves, more time can be spent on quality instruction that impacts a greater percentage of the overall student population.
Implementation:	This objective is best implemented by constant staff modeling, coaching, and support for all students.

Jump-start Objective - Planning and Tracking Tool

Jump-start Objective: *Our school will decrease the number of office referrals.*

Target: _____

Initial Data: _____

Measurement Cycle: _____

Initial Improvement Action(s)

- Action 1: _____
- Action 2: _____
- Action 3: _____

1st Check Point (____ / ____ / ____)

- Check Point Results: _____
- Revised Action(s): _____

2nd Check Point (____ / ____ / ____)

- Check Point Results: _____
- Revised Action(s): _____

3rd Check Point (____ / ____ / ____)

- Check Point Results: _____
- Revised Action(s): _____

4th Check Point (____ / ____ / ____)

- **Check Point Results:** _____
- **Revised Action(s):** _____

5th Check Point (____ / ____ / ____)

- **Check Point Results:** _____
- **Revised Action(s):** _____

6th Check Point (____ / ____ / ____)

- **Check Point Results:** _____
- **Revised Action(s):** _____

Responsible Parties:

_____
_____
_____
_____
_____
_____

Objective #2: Discipline and Behavior

Our school will increase the number of students who receive campus-wide recognition for positive behaviors.

Objective Target:	At least a 15 percent increase in the number of students recognized should be selected.
Measurement Cycle:	Select three weeks, four weeks, six weeks, or nine weeks.
Campus Levels:	This objective is appropriate for campuses serving any grade level.
Why:	The positive adult practices and school systems that increase the incidents of positive student behavior also support increased student performance (McClure & Spector, 1997).
Power:	Reducing discipline referrals is a measure of the absence of a behavior. On the other hand, increasing positive rewards is a measure of increasing desirable behaviors.

Implementation: This objective is best implemented by constant staff modeling, coaching, and support for all students.

Jump-start Objective - Planning and Tracking Tool

Jump-start Objective: *Our school will increase the number of students who receive campus-wide recognition for positive behaviors.*

Target: _____

Initial Data: _____

Measurement Cycle: _____

Initial Improvement Action(s)

- Action 1:_____
- Action 2:_____
- Action 3:_____

1st Check Point (____ / ____ / ____)

- Check Point Results:_____
- Revised Action(s): _____

2nd Check Point (____ / ____ / ____)

- Check Point Results:_____
- Revised Action(s): _____

3rd Check Point (____ / ____ / ____)

- **Check Point Results:**_____

- **Revised Action(s):** _____

4th Check Point (____ / ____ / ____)

- **Check Point Results:**_____

- **Revised Action(s):** _____

5th Check Point (____ / ____ / ____)

- **Check Point Results:**_____

- **Revised Action(s):** _____

6th Check Point (____ / ____ / ____)

- **Check Point Results:**_____

- **Revised Action(s):** _____

Responsible Parties:

_____
_____
_____
_____
_____
_____

Objective #3: Discipline and Behavior

Our school will reduce the daily frequency of "late to school" incidents.

Objective Target:	At least a 15 percent decrease in the number of students arriving late should be selected.
Measurement Cycle:	Select three weeks, four weeks, or six weeks.
Campus Levels:	This objective is appropriate for campuses serving any grade level.
Why:	The author has observed that the culture that allows "late to school" behavior to become a norm, becomes an impediment to achieving at high levels. When the practice becomes accepted, it communicates that the school does not do anything of real importance in the morning.
Power:	Getting school started at full speed creates a sense of purpose and urgency.

Implementation: There are three critical steps to implementing this objective. First, communicate and enforce the rule that "late, plus an excuse, equals late." Second, make sure that important things occur at the start of school. Third, insist that teachers begin their instruction as soon as the first bell rings.

JUMP START YOUR SCHOOL!

Jump-start Objective - Planning and Tracking Tool

Jump-start Objective: *Our school will reduce the daily frequency of "late to school" incidents.*

Target: _____

Initial Data: _____

Measurement Cycle: _____

Initial Improvement Action(s)

- **Action 1:** _____
- **Action 2:** _____
- **Action 3:** _____

1ˢᵗ **Check Point (** ____ / ____ / ____ **)**

- **Check Point Results:** _____
- **Revised Action(s):** _____

2ⁿᵈ **Check Point (** ____ / ____ / ____ **)**

- **Check Point Results:** _____
- **Revised Action(s):** _____

3rd Check Point (____ / ____ / ____)

- **Check Point Results:**_____
- **Revised Action(s):** _____

4th Check Point (____ / ____ / ____)

- **Check Point Results:**_____
- **Revised Action(s):** _____

5th Check Point (____ / ____ / ____)

- **Check Point Results:**_____
- **Revised Action(s):** _____

6th Check Point (____ / ____ / ____)

- **Check Point Results:**_____
- **Revised Action(s):** _____

Responsible Parties:

_____
_____
_____
_____
_____
_____

Objective #4: Discipline and Behavior

Our school will increase student attendance rates.

Objective Target:	A target attendance rate in the mid to high 90 percent range should be selected unless the current attendance rate is less than 85 percent. If that is the case, the target should represent at least an 8 percentage point gain. If the current campus attendance rate is currently above 96.5 percent, select a different objective, as attendance is not a significant issue faced by the campus.
Measurement Cycle:	Select one week, three weeks, or four weeks.
Campus Levels:	This objective is appropriate for campuses serving any grade level.
Why:	Students are not receiving quality instruction when they are not in school.

Power:	One of the first rules of improved student performance is that even poor instruction is better than no instruction. Just getting students in class more often improves results.
Implementation:	Increasing attendance is about the use of carrots, sticks, and immediate action. Carrots (incentives and rewards) are more powerful when used often and at short intervals. Sticks (any punitive action) must be used as soon as an attendance problem is identified. The longer the problem is allowed to fester without corrective action, the more difficult it is to change the behavior.

Jump-start Objective - Planning and Tracking Tool

Jump-start Objective: *Our school will increase student attendance rates.*

Target: _____

Initial Data: _____

Measurement Cycle: _____

Initial Improvement Action(s)

- Action 1:_____
- Action 2:_____
- Action 3:_____

1st Check Point (____ / ____ / ____)

- Check Point Results:_____
- Revised Action(s): _____

2nd Check Point (____ / ____ / ____)

- Check Point Results:_____
- Revised Action(s): _____

3rd Check Point (____ / ____ / ____)

- Check Point Results:_____
- Revised Action(s): _____

4ᵗʰ Check Point (____ / ____ / ____)

- **Check Point Results:** _____
- **Revised Action(s):** _____

5ᵗʰ Check Point (____ / ____ / ____)

- **Check Point Results:** _____
- **Revised Action(s):** _____

6ᵗʰ Check Point (____ / ____ / ____)

- **Check Point Results:** _____
- **Revised Action(s):** _____

Responsible Parties:

_____
_____
_____
_____
_____
_____

Objective #5: Discipline and Behavior

Our school will decrease the incidents of vandalism and graffiti.

Objective Target:	At least a 15 percent decrease in vandalism and graffiti should be selected.
Measurement Cycle:	Select one week, three weeks, or six weeks.
Campus Levels:	This objective is appropriate for campuses serving any grade level.
Why:	The author has observed that visible vandalism and graffiti has a depressing effect on campus morale and performance. It communicates a lack of attention and purpose.
Power:	Immediately repairing vandalism and cleaning up graffiti communicates that the campus is safe, orderly, and secure and that the business of school and student learning is important.

Implementation:	This objective is best implemented through constant vigilance, maintenance, and service learning projects.

Jump-start Objective - Planning and Tracking Tool

Jump-start Objective: *Our school will decrease the incidents of vandalism and graffiti.*

Target: _____

Initial Data: _____

Measurement Cycle: _____

Initial Improvement Action(s)

- Action 1:_____
- Action 2:_____
- Action 3:_____

1st Check Point (___ / ___ / ___)

- **Check Point Results:**_____
- **Revised Action(s):** _____

2nd Check Point (___ / ___ / ___)

- **Check Point Results:**_____
- **Revised Action(s):** _____

3rd Check Point (____ / ____ / ____)

- **Check Point Results:**_____
- **Revised Action(s):** _____

4th Check Point (____ / ____ / ____)

- **Check Point Results:**_____
- **Revised Action(s):** _____

5th Check Point (____ / ____ / ____)

- **Check Point Results:**_____
- **Revised Action(s):** _____

6th Check Point (____ / ____ / ____)

- **Check Point Results:**_____
- **Revised Action(s):** _____

Responsible Parties:

_____
_____
_____
_____
_____
_____

Objective #6: Discipline and Behavior

Our school will reduce the number of in-school and out-of-school suspensions.

Objective Target:	At least a 25 percent decrease in in-school and out-of-school suspensions should be selected.
Measurement Cycle:	Select six weeks, nine weeks, or a semester.
Campus Levels:	This objective is appropriate for campuses serving any grade level.
Why:	As addressed in a previous objective, even poor instruction is better than no instruction. Suspended students receive nothing that resembles quality instruction.
Power:	Keeping more students in class and productive has a significant positive impact on campus performance.

Implementation:	This objective is best implemented through the use of a reasonable, pro-active discipline continuum and changing suspension practices. It has been the author's experience that any out-of-school suspension longer than one and a half days is counterproductive, both behaviorally and academically.

Jump-start Objective - Planning and Tracking Tool

Jump-start Objective: *Our school will reduce the number of in-school and out-of-school suspensions.*

Target: _____

Initial Data: _____

Measurement Cycle: _____

Initial Improvement Action(s)

- **Action 1:** _____
- **Action 2:** _____
- **Action 3:** _____

1st Check Point (____ / ____ / ____ **)**

- **Check Point Results:** _____
- **Revised Action(s):** _____

2nd Check Point (____ / ____ / ____ **)**

- **Check Point Results:** _____
- **Revised Action(s):** _____

3ʳᵈ Check Point (____ / ____ / ____)

- **Check Point Results:**_____
- **Revised Action(s):** _____

4ᵗʰ Check Point (____ / ____ / ____)

- **Check Point Results:**_____
- **Revised Action(s):** _____

5ᵗʰ Check Point (____ / ____ / ____)

- **Check Point Results:**_____
- **Revised Action(s):** _____

6ᵗʰ Check Point (____ / ____ / ____)

- **Check Point Results:**_____
- **Revised Action(s):** _____

Responsible Parties:

_____
_____
_____
_____
_____
_____

Objective #7: Discipline and Behavior

Our school will reduce Discipline Alternative Education Program (off-campus placement) referrals.

Objective Target:	At least a 20 percent decrease in off-campus placements should be selected.
Measurement Cycle:	Select six weeks, nine weeks, or a semester.
Campus Levels:	This objective is appropriate for campuses serving any grade level.
Why:	No matter how good the quality of instruction is in discipline programs, it still pales in comparison to the quality of instruction that is provided in the regular classroom.
Power:	Keeping more students on campus and productive has a significant positive impact on campus performance.

Implementation: This objective is best implemented through the use of a reasonable, pro-active discipline continuum, improved staff supervision, and student mentoring.

Jump-start Objective - Planning and Tracking Tool

Jump-start Objective: *Our school will reduce Discipline Alternative Education Program (off-campus placement) referrals.*

Target: _____

Initial Data: _____

Measurement Cycle: _____

Initial Improvement Action(s)

- Action 1: _____
- Action 2: _____
- Action 3: _____

1st Check Point (____ / ____ / ____)

- Check Point Results: _____
- Revised Action(s): _____

2nd Check Point (____ / ____ / ____)

- Check Point Results: _____
- Revised Action(s): _____

3rd Check Point (____ / ____ / ____)

- **Check Point Results:** _____
- **Revised Action(s):** _____

4th Check Point (____ / ____ / ____)

- **Check Point Results:** _____
- **Revised Action(s):** _____

5th Check Point (____ / ____ / ____)

- **Check Point Results:** _____
- **Revised Action(s):** _____

6th Check Point (____ / ____ / ____)

- **Check Point Results:** _____
- **Revised Action(s):** _____

Responsible Parties:

_____
_____
_____
_____
_____
_____

Chapter 3: Instructional Rigor and Relevance

Many experts agree that instructional rigor and relevance is where the rubber meets the road for increased student performance. In a number of his presentations, Dr. Willard Daggett, of the *International Center for Leadership in Education*, makes an excellent case that increasing the level of instructional rigor and relevance is paramount to ensuring that the United States remains a world economic leader. His *Rigor/Relevance Framework*™ provides a powerful lesson design tool that both individuals and teams of teachers are using to create more meaningful lessons and activities in support of this belief (for more information, visit www.leadered.com).

As a school leader and educator, one can spend countless days trying to tweak the system and make cosmetic changes to a campus, but if classroom instruction is ignored, everything else risks becoming nothing but busy work. More and more, experts and cutting-edge practitioners, such as E. Don Brown (past president, National Association of Secondary School Principals) and Dr. Thomas Price and Dr. Michael Laird (Splendora Independent School District, Texas) argue that improving classroom instruction and ramping up rigor and relevance is the alpha and omega of improved student performance.

During the course of introductory meetings with the author, many principals express the belief that they are primarily responsible for campus and administrative procedures, and teachers are almost solely responsible for instruction. This may have been true in the era before accountability and an exponentially increasing knowledge base, but today, this belief is not only debilitating to a campus, it is simply wrong. It is now becoming evident that, on campuses that are beginning to experience significant gains in student performance, everyone is responsible for instruction, especially leadership. Only leadership is uniquely positioned to see larger trends and leverage resources. When this responsibility is either ignored or abdicated, both students and teachers suffer.

Understand that instructional rigor and relevance is not specifically about harder work, it is about creating deeper understanding that lends itself to tasks that are more complex. It is about teachers changing the way they teach in order to get more students to those deeper understanding levels. It is about the excitement and thrill of teaching and learning.

Because instructional rigor and relevance is what school is really about, this is the largest chapter in this book. Included are fourteen short-term objectives that focus the campus on dramatically increasing the rigor and relevance of classroom instruction. The power of these objectives is that by necessity, this focus must extend beyond the advanced classroom and begin to permeate in every class and impact every student. It is by increasing the overall quality of instruction in every classroom that a school can virtually guarantee that the performance of all students will be impacted positively.

Objective #8: Instructional Rigor and Relevance

Our school will increase enrollment in AVID classes.

AVID:	*Advancement via Individual Determination. AVID is an elective course that is designed to prepare B, C, and D students for the requirements and expectations of a four-year college. AVID classes can be offered in grades four through twelve. For more information, visit www.avidonline.org.*
Objective Target:	Select at least a 25 percent increase in enrolment. Many campuses see increases in excess of 100 percent in the first year of focusing on this objective.
Measurement Cycle:	Select semester.
Campus Levels:	This objective is appropriate for any campus serving students in grades four through twelve.

Why:	Many current school leaders believe that AVID provides students with critical skills that support success in more rigorous academic courses.
Power:	On many campuses, AVID is often a precursor to increased pre-advanced placement (AP), AP, and dual-credit enrollment. Proponents of the program believe that it increases the chances of its participants both enrolling and successfully remaining in college.
Implementation:	This objective can be implemented through aggressive school counseling and an overall campus focus on continuing education.

Jump-start Objective - Planning and Tracking Tool

Jump-start Objective: *Our school will increase enrollment in AVID classes.*

Target: _____

Initial Data: _____

Measurement Cycle: _____

Initial Improvement Action(s)

- Action 1:_____
- Action 2:_____
- Action 3:_____

1st Check Point (____ / ____ / ____)

- Check Point Results:_____
- Revised Action(s): _____

2nd Check Point (____ / ____ / ____)

- Check Point Results:_____
- Revised Action(s): _____

3rd Check Point (____ / ____ / ____)

- Check Point Results:_____
- Revised Action(s): _____

4th **Check Point (** ____ / ____ / ____ **)**

- **Check Point Results:**_____
- **Revised Action(s):** _____

5th **Check Point (** ____ / ____ / ____ **)**

- **Check Point Results:**_____
- **Revised Action(s):** _____

6th **Check Point (** ____ / ____ / ____ **)**

- **Check Point Results:**_____
- **Revised Action(s):** _____

Responsible Parties:

_____
_____
_____
_____
_____
_____

Objective #9: Instructional Rigor and Relevance

Our school will increase enrollment in pre-AP courses.

Objective Target:	An increase in enrollment of at least 15 percent should be selected.
Measurement Cycle:	Select semester.
Campus Levels:	This objective is appropriate for secondary campuses.
Why:	The author has observed that increasing the number of students experiencing success in more rigorous courses enhances the academic culture and climate of the campus.
Power:	Many campuses report that increased enrollment in pre-AP courses leads to an increase in enrollment in AP courses.
Implementation:	This objective can be implemented through recruiting and a campus focus on increasing rigor for all students.

Jump-start Objective - Planning and Tracking Tool

Jump-start Objective: *Our school will increase enrollment in pre-AP courses.*

Target: _____

Initial Data: _____

Measurement Cycle: _____

Initial Improvement Action(s)

- **Action 1:** _____
- **Action 2:** _____
- **Action 3:** _____

1st Check Point (____ / ____ / ____)

- **Check Point Results:** _____
- **Revised Action(s):** _____

2nd Check Point (____ / ____ / ____)

- **Check Point Results:** _____
- **Revised Action(s):** _____

3rd Check Point (____ / ____ / ____)

- **Check Point Results:** _____
- **Revised Action(s):** _____

4th Check Point (____ / ____ / ____)

- **Check Point Results:**_____

- **Revised Action(s):** _____

5th Check Point (____ / ____ / ____)

- **Check Point Results:**_____

- **Revised Action(s):** _____

6th Check Point (____ / ____ / ____)

- **Check Point Results:**_____

- **Revised Action(s):** _____

Responsible Parties:

_____
_____
_____
_____
_____
_____
_____

Objective #10: Instructional Rigor and Relevance

Our school will increase the number of students enrolled in advanced classes.

Objective Target:	An increase in enrollment of at least 15 percent should be selected.
Measurement Cycle:	Select semester.
Campus Levels:	This objective is appropriate for secondary campuses.
Why:	The author has observed that increasing the number of students experiencing success in more rigorous courses enhances the academic culture and climate of the campus.
Power:	The author has observed that the drive to ensure the success of more students in more rigorous courses lends itself to more frequent and effective use of instructional best practices.

Implementation:	This objective can be implemented through recruiting and a campus focus on increasing rigor for all students.

Jump-start Objective - Planning and Tracking Tool

Jump-start Objective: *Our school will increase the number of students enrolled in advanced classes.*

Target: _____

Initial Data: _____

Measurement Cycle: _____

Initial Improvement Action(s)

- Action 1:_____
- Action 2:_____
- Action 3:_____

1st Check Point (____ / ____ / ____)

- **Check Point Results:**_____
- **Revised Action(s):** _____

2nd Check Point (____ / ____ / ____)

- **Check Point Results:**_____
- **Revised Action(s):** _____

3rd Check Point (____ / ____ / ____)

- **Check Point Results:** _____
- **Revised Action(s):** _____

4th Check Point (____ / ____ / ____)

- **Check Point Results:** _____
- **Revised Action(s):** _____

5th Check Point (____ / ____ / ____)

- **Check Point Results:** _____
- **Revised Action(s):** _____

6th Check Point (____ / ____ / ____)

- **Check Point Results:** _____
- **Revised Action(s):** _____

Responsible Parties:

_____
_____
_____
_____
_____
_____

Objective #11: Instructional Rigor and Relevance

Our school will increase the total number of students enrolled in dual-credit courses.

Dual-credit Course: *A course taken by a student in which the student earns both high school and college credit. Dual-credit courses are generally taken either at the high school, at the college, or on-line. For more information, contact your state education agency and/or local colleges.*

Objective Target: An increase in enrollment of at least 10 percent should be selected.

Measurement Cycle: Select semester.

Campus Levels: This objective is appropriate for secondary campuses.

Why: Dual-credit courses offer increased academic rigor with the added benefit of students earning college credit while still enrolled in high school.

Power:	The ability to earn college credits while still in high school makes college more accessible and affordable for students.
Implementation:	This objective can be implemented through recruiting, a campus focus on increasing rigor for all students, and partnerships with institutions of higher learning.

Jump-start Objective - Planning and Tracking Tool

Jump-start Objective: *Our school will increase the total number of students enrolled in dual-credit courses.*

Target: _____

Initial Data: _____

Measurement Cycle: _____

Initial Improvement Action(s)

- Action 1:_____
- Action 2:_____
- Action 3:_____

1st Check Point (____ / ____ / ____)

- Check Point Results:_____
- Revised Action(s): _____

2nd Check Point (____ / ____ / ____)

- Check Point Results:_____
- Revised Action(s): _____

3rd Check Point (____ / ____ / ____)

- **Check Point Results:** _____

- **Revised Action(s):** _____

4th Check Point (____ / ____ / ____)

- **Check Point Results:** _____

- **Revised Action(s):** _____

5th Check Point (____ / ____ / ____)

- **Check Point Results:** _____

- **Revised Action(s):** _____

6th Check Point (____ / ____ / ____)

- **Check Point Results:** _____

- **Revised Action(s):** _____

Responsible Parties:

_____
_____
_____
_____
_____
_____

Objective #12: Instructional Rigor and Relevance

Our school will increase the number of students enrolled in AP courses.

AP Course:	*One of 37 courses that a high school student can enroll in that is aligned with and prepares the student to take an AP exam. Many colleges give students varying levels of additional credit based on AP exam results. For more information, visit www.collegeboard.com/student/testing/ap/about.html.*
Objective Target:	An increase in enrollment of at least 10 percent should be selected.
Measurement Cycle:	Select semester.
Campus Levels:	This objective is appropriate for secondary campuses.
Why:	The author has observed that increasing the number of students experiencing success in more rigorous courses enhances the academic culture and climate of the campus.

Power:	Success in AP courses is correlated to increased chances of success in college (Geiser, 2008).
Implementation:	This objective can be implemented through recruiting and a campus focus on increasing rigor for all students.

Jump-start Objective - Planning and Tracking Tool

Jump-start Objective: *Our school will increase the number of students enrolled in AP courses.*

Target: _____

Initial Data: _____

Measurement Cycle: _____

Initial Improvement Action(s)

- **Action 1:**_____
- **Action 2:**_____
- **Action 3:**_____

1st Check Point (____ / ____ / ____)

- **Check Point Results:**_____
- **Revised Action(s):** _____

2nd Check Point (____ / ____ / ____)

- **Check Point Results:**_____
- **Revised Action(s):** _____

3ʳᵈ Check Point (____ / ____ / ____)

- **Check Point Results:**_____

- **Revised Action(s):** _____

4ᵗʰ Check Point (____ / ____ / ____)

- **Check Point Results:**_____

- **Revised Action(s):** _____

5ᵗʰ Check Point (____ / ____ / ____)

- **Check Point Results:**_____

- **Revised Action(s):** _____

6ᵗʰ Check Point (____ / ____ / ____)

- **Check Point Results:**_____

- **Revised Action(s):** _____

Responsible Parties:

_____
_____
_____
_____
_____
_____

Objective #13: Instructional Rigor and Relevance

Our school will increase the percentage of students passing AP exams.

Objective Target: This target is dependent on the number of students that currently do not take, or do not pass, the AP exams. The greater the number of students that fit in these categories, the more aggressive the selected target should be. Choose between a 10 percent to a 100 percent increase in the number of students passing the exams.

Measurement Cycle: Annual. This is the only annual objective presented in this book. If this objective is chosen, another objective should also be selected because AP tests are only conducted once a year.

Campus Levels: This objective is appropriate for secondary campuses.

Why:	The result achieved on an AP exam is generally considered the best measure of success in an AP course.
Power:	Success in AP courses is correlated to increased chances of success in college (Geiser, 2008).
Implementation:	This objective can be implemented through improved instructional practices and timely student academic interventions.

Jump-start Objective - Planning and Tracking Tool

Jump-start Objective: *Our school will increase the percentage of students passing AP exams.*

Target: _____

Initial Data: _____

Measurement Cycle: _____

Initial Improvement Action(s)

- Action 1:_____
- Action 2:_____
- Action 3:_____

1st Check Point (____ / ____ / ____)

- **Check Point Results:**_____
- **Revised Action(s):** _____

2nd Check Point (____ / ____ / ____)

- **Check Point Results:**_____
- **Revised Action(s):** _____

3rd Check Point (____ / ____ / ____)

- **Check Point Results:**_____
- **Revised Action(s):** _____

4th Check Point (____ / ____ / ____)

- **Check Point Results:**_____
- **Revised Action(s):** _____

5th Check Point (____ / ____ / ____)

- **Check Point Results:**_____
- **Revised Action(s):** _____

6th Check Point (____ / ____ / ____)

- **Check Point Results:**_____
- **Revised Action(s):** _____

Responsible Parties:

_____
_____
_____
_____
_____
_____

Objective #14: Instructional Rigor and Relevance

Our school will increase the observed level of students who are engaged in the use of Socratic questioning strategies.

Socratic Questioning: *Socratic questioning is one of the oldest strategies for provoking critical thinking by students. It is a teaching technique in which the original question is treated as it were the answer. This leads to deeper discussions and better understanding as the discourse continues. Some simple examples of Socratic questions are, "What is a measureable objective," and "Why is a measurable objective important?"*

Objective Target: An increase of 2 percent to 5 percent of the number of students observed engaged in the Socratic questioning process, per measurement cycle, should be selected.

Measurement Cycle: Select two weeks, three weeks, four weeks, or six weeks.

Campus Levels:	This objective is appropriate for campuses serving any grade level.
Why:	Proponents of the strategy report that the increased use of Socratic questioning is one way to improve the overall quality of classroom instruction.
Power:	The appropriate use of Socratic questioning can increase academic rigor.
Implementation:	This objective can be implemented through professional development, increased team planning by teachers, and the hyper-monitoring of instruction.

Hyper-monitoring: The practice of professional support staff conducting twenty to twenty-five classroom observations each week, using a common walk-thru protocol, such as PowerWalks. The purpose of this practice is to provide the entire campus with objective data on the current quality of instruction. The author is a pioneer of this concept. For more information visit the Lead Your School website at www.leadyourschool.com.

Jump-start Objective - Planning and Tracking Tool

Jump-start Objective: *Our school will increase the observed level of students who are engaged in the use of Socratic questioning strategies.*

Target: _____

Initial Data: _____

Measurement Cycle: _____

Initial Improvement Action(s)

- **Action 1:** _____
- **Action 2:** _____
- **Action 3:** _____

1ˢᵗ Check Point (____ / ____ / ____)

- **Check Point Results:** _____
- **Revised Action(s):** _____

2ⁿᵈ Check Point (____ / ____ / ____)

- **Check Point Results:** _____
- **Revised Action(s):** _____

3rd Check Point (____ / ____ / ____)

- **Check Point Results:**_____
- **Revised Action(s):** _____

4th Check Point (____ / ____ / ____)

- **Check Point Results:**_____
- **Revised Action(s):** _____

5th Check Point (____ / ____ / ____)

- **Check Point Results:**_____
- **Revised Action(s):** _____

6th Check Point (____ / ____ / ____)

- **Check Point Results:**_____
- **Revised Action(s):** _____

Responsible Parties:

_____
_____
_____
_____
_____
_____

Objective #15: Instructional Rigor and Relevance

Our school will increase the observed level of students who are working at the application level or higher on Bloom's taxonomy.

Objective Target:	An increase of 2 percent to 5 percent of the number of students observed working at the application level or higher, per measurement cycle, should be selected.
Measurement Cycle:	Select two weeks, three weeks, four weeks, or six weeks.
Campus Levels:	This objective is appropriate for campuses serving any grade level.
Why:	The author has observed that instruction at the higher levels of Bloom's taxonomy often increases the relevance of the lesson and student engagement.

Power:	As the quality of instruction improves, there is a correlated increase in student performance (Marzano, Pickering, & Pollock, 2004).
Implementation:	This objective can be implemented through professional development, increased team planning by teachers, and the hyper-monitoring of instruction.

Jump-start Objective - Planning and Tracking Tool

Jump-start Objective: *Our school will increase the observed level of students who are working at the application level or higher on Bloom's taxonomy.*

Target: _____

Initial Data: _____

Measurement Cycle: _____

Initial Improvement Action(s)

- **Action 1:** _____
- **Action 2:** _____
- **Action 3:** _____

1st Check Point (____ / ____ / ____)

- **Check Point Results:** _____
- **Revised Action(s):** _____

2nd Check Point (____ / ____ / ____)

- **Check Point Results:** _____
- **Revised Action(s):** _____

3rd Check Point (____ / ____ / ____)

    • **Check Point Results:**_____

    • **Revised Action(s):** _____

4th Check Point (____ / ____ / ____)

    • **Check Point Results:**_____

    • **Revised Action(s):** _____

5th Check Point (____ / ____ / ____)

    • **Check Point Results:**_____

    • **Revised Action(s):** _____

6th Check Point (____ / ____ / ____)

    • **Check Point Results:**_____

    • **Revised Action(s):** _____

Responsible Parties:

_____
_____
_____
_____
_____
_____

Objective #16: Instructional Rigor and Relevance

Our school will increase the observed level of students who are participating in cooperative learning and small group instructional activities.

Objective Target:	An increase of 2 percent to 5 percent of the number of students observed participating in cooperative learning and/or small group activities, per measurement cycle, should be selected.
Measurement Cycle:	Select two weeks, three weeks, four weeks, or six weeks.
Campus Levels:	This objective is appropriate for campuses serving any grade level.
Why:	Many practitioners believe that students build meaning and understanding more rapidly when working with teams or in small groups.

Power: Many practitioners believe that the increased use of collaborative learning and small group activities often has the added benefit of improving student communication skills.

Implementation: This objective can be implemented through professional development, increased team planning by teachers, and the hyper-monitoring of instruction.

Jump-start Objective - Planning and Tracking Tool

Jump-start Objective: *Our school will increase the observed level of students who are participating in cooperative learning and small group instructional activities.*

Target: _____

Initial Data: _____

Measurement Cycle: _____

Initial Improvement Action(s)

- Action 1:_____
- Action 2:_____
- Action 3:_____

1st Check Point (____ / ____ / ____)

- Check Point Results:_____
- Revised Action(s): _____

2nd Check Point (____ / ____ / ____)

- Check Point Results:_____
- Revised Action(s): _____

3rd Check Point (____ / ____ / ____)

- **Check Point Results:**_____

- **Revised Action(s):** _____

4th Check Point (____ / ____ / ____)

- **Check Point Results:**_____

- **Revised Action(s):** _____

5th Check Point (____ / ____ / ____)

- **Check Point Results:**_____

- **Revised Action(s):** _____

6th Check Point (____ / ____ / ____)

- **Check Point Results:**_____

- **Revised Action(s):** _____

Responsible Parties:

_____
_____
_____
_____
_____
_____

Objective #17: Instructional Rigor and Relevance

Our school will increase the amount of reflective writing required in each core course.

Objective Target:	At least one reflective writing assignment, per course, should be required each week.
Measurement Cycle:	Select one week, three weeks, four weeks, or six weeks.
Campus Levels:	This objective is appropriate for campuses serving any grade level.
Why:	A number of teachers believe that the use of reflective writing increases learning connections, personalized meaning, and retention of key concepts and ideas.
Power:	Writing proficiency is correlated to improved reading and mathematics performance (Parker, Louie, & O'Dwyer, 2009).

Implementation: This objective can be implemented through professional development and increased team planning by teachers.

JUMP START YOUR SCHOOL!

Jump-start Objective - Planning and Tracking Tool

Jump-start Objective: *Our school will increase the amount of reflective writing required in each core course.*

Target: _____

Initial Data: _____

Measurement Cycle: _____

Initial Improvement Action(s)

- **Action 1:** _____
- **Action 2:** _____
- **Action 3:** _____

1st Check Point (____ / ____ / ____)

- **Check Point Results:** _____
- **Revised Action(s):** _____

2nd Check Point (____ / ____ / ____)

- **Check Point Results:** _____
- **Revised Action(s):** _____

3rd Check Point (____ / ____ / ____)

- **Check Point Results:**_____

- **Revised Action(s):** _____

4th Check Point (____ / ____ / ____)

- **Check Point Results:**_____

- **Revised Action(s):** _____

5th Check Point (____ / ____ / ____)

- **Check Point Results:**_____

- **Revised Action(s):** _____

6th Check Point (____ / ____ / ____)

- **Check Point Results:**_____

- **Revised Action(s):** _____

Responsible Parties:

_____
_____
_____
_____
_____
_____

Objective #18: Instructional Rigor and Relevance

Our school will increase student performance on interdisciplinary group projects.

Objective Target:	On the group project, 80 percent of students will score 80 percent or higher, based on a pre-determined rubric.*
	The lowest recommended target.
Measurement Cycle:	Select six weeks, nine weeks, twelve weeks, or a semester.
Campus Levels:	This objective is appropriate for campuses serving any grade level.
Why:	Engaging in interdisciplinary activities is one way to increase both the relevance and rigor of instruction.

Power:	Based on the data generated from over seventeen thousand classroom observations, the use of interdisciplinary instructional activities is the most underused teaching best practice. This is in spite of the fact that most teachers agree that the use of interdisciplinary activities is a critical component in increasing course relevance (Cain, 2009).
Implementation:	An easy way to achieve this objective is to schedule one project per quarter and have teams of teachers design the project rubric prior to the activity.

Jump-start Objective - Planning and Tracking Tool

Jump-start Objective: *Our school will increase student performance on interdisciplinary group projects.*

Target: _____

Initial Data: _____

Measurement Cycle: _____

Initial Improvement Action(s)

- Action 1:_____
- Action 2:_____
- Action 3:_____

1st Check Point (____ / ____ / ____)

- Check Point Results:_____
- Revised Action(s): _____

2nd Check Point (____ / ____ / ____)

- Check Point Results:_____
- Revised Action(s): _____

3rd Check Point (____ / ____ / ____)

- Check Point Results:_____

- Revised Action(s): _____

4th Check Point (____ / ____ / ____)

- Check Point Results:_____

- Revised Action(s): _____

5th Check Point (____ / ____ / ____)

- Check Point Results:_____

- Revised Action(s): _____

6th Check Point (____ / ____ / ____)

- Check Point Results:_____

- Revised Action(s): _____

Responsible Parties:

_____
_____
_____
_____
_____
_____

Objective #19: Instructional Rigor and Relevance

Our school will increase student performance on multi-media research projects.

Objective Target:	On the research project, 80 percent of students will score 80 percent or higher, based on a pre-determined rubric.*
	* The lowest recommended target.
Measurement Cycle:	Select nine weeks, twelve weeks, or a semester.
Campus Levels:	This objective is appropriate for campuses serving any grade level.
Why:	The ability to integrate technology effectively into academic endeavors is being recognized as a critical life-long learning skill.
Power:	The author has observed that the exposure to and use of technology can increase instructional relevance and student engagement.

Implementation: An easy way to achieve this objective is to schedule one project per quarter and have teams of teachers design the project rubric prior to the activity.

Jump-start Objective - Planning and Tracking Tool

Jump-start Objective: *Our school will increase student performance on multi-media research projects.*

Target: _____

Initial Data: _____

Measurement Cycle: _____

Initial Improvement Action(s)

- Action 1: _____
- Action 2: _____
- Action 3: _____

1st Check Point (____ / ____ / ____)

- **Check Point Results:** _____
- **Revised Action(s):** _____

2nd Check Point (____ / ____ / ____)

- **Check Point Results:** _____
- **Revised Action(s):** _____

3rd Check Point (____ / ____ / ____)

- Check Point Results:_____
- Revised Action(s): _____

4th Check Point (____ / ____ / ____)

- Check Point Results:_____
- Revised Action(s): _____

5th Check Point (____ / ____ / ____)

- Check Point Results:_____
- Revised Action(s): _____

6th Check Point (____ / ____ / ____)

- Check Point Results:_____
- Revised Action(s): _____

Responsible Parties:

_____
_____
_____
_____
_____
_____

Objective #20: Instructional Rigor and Relevance

Our school will increase the observed number of students using the Cornell Notes process.

Cornell Notes process: *A structured and specific way to take class notes designed to facilitate retention and test taking performance. For more information, web search "Cornell Notes."*

Objective Target: An increase of 2 percent to 5 percent in the number of students using the Cornell Notes process, per measurement cycle, should be selected.

Measurement Cycle: Select two weeks, three weeks, four weeks, or six weeks.

Campus Levels: This objective is appropriate for campuses serving any grade level.

Why: The practice of note taking allows students to express concepts in their own terms, which many educators believe increases retention.

Power:	Note taking has been identified as one of the most effective teaching strategies (Marzano, Pickering, & Pollock, 2004; Schmoker, 2006).
Implementation:	This objective can be implemented through professional development, increased team planning by teachers, and the hyper-monitoring of instruction.

Jump-start Objective - Planning and Tracking Tool

Jump-start Objective: *Our school will increase the observed number of students using the Cornell Notes process.*

Target: _____

Initial Data: _____

Measurement Cycle: _____

Initial Improvement Action(s)

- **Action 1:**_____
- **Action 2:**_____
- **Action 3:**_____

1st **Check Point** (____ / ____ / ____)

- **Check Point Results:**_____
- **Revised Action(s):** _____

2nd **Check Point** (____ / ____ / ____)

- **Check Point Results:**_____
- **Revised Action(s):** _____

3rd Check Point (____ / ____ / ____)

- **Check Point Results:** _____
- **Revised Action(s):** _____

4th Check Point (____ / ____ / ____)

- **Check Point Results:** _____
- **Revised Action(s):** _____

5th Check Point (____ / ____ / ____)

- **Check Point Results:** _____
- **Revised Action(s):** _____

6th Check Point (____ / ____ / ____)

- **Check Point Results:** _____
- **Revised Action(s):** _____

Responsible Parties:

_____
_____
_____
_____
_____
_____

Objective #21: Instructional Rigor and Relevance

Our school will increase student writing performance.

Objective Target:	On common writing prompts, 80 percent of students will score 80 percent or higher, based on a pre-determined rubric.*
	The lowest recommended target.
Measurement Cycle:	Select three weeks, four weeks, or six weeks.
Campus Levels:	This objective is appropriate for campuses serving any grade level.
Why:	The ability to write effectively is correlated to literacy skills. Many experts believe that writing is a critical component in the ability to think critically (Parker, Louie, & O'Dwyer, 2009).

Power:	The ability to communicate effectively is a critical skill that many employers look for when making hiring decisions.
Implementation:	An easy way to achieve this objective is to have a campus wide writing prompt that is used by all English classes on the same day. Have teams of teachers design the grading rubric and then teach the rubric to students.

Jump-start Objective - Planning and Tracking Tool

Jump-start Objective: *Our school will increase student writing performance.*

Target: _____

Initial Data: _____

Measurement Cycle: _____

Initial Improvement Action(s)

- Action 1:_____
- Action 2:_____
- Action 3:_____

1st Check Point (____ / ____ / ____)

- Check Point Results:_____
- Revised Action(s): _____

2nd Check Point (____ / ____ / ____)

- Check Point Results:_____
- Revised Action(s): _____

3rd Check Point (_____ / _____ / _____)

  • **Check Point Results:** _____

  • **Revised Action(s):** _____

4th Check Point (_____ / _____ / _____)

  • **Check Point Results:** _____

  • **Revised Action(s):** _____

5th Check Point (_____ / _____ / _____)

  • **Check Point Results:** _____

  • **Revised Action(s):** _____

6th Check Point (_____ / _____ / _____)

  • **Check Point Results:** _____

  • **Revised Action(s):** _____

Responsible Parties:

_____
_____
_____
_____
_____
_____

Chapter 4: Literacy

Improving student literacy competence is the aspirin of education. It makes every classroom operate better. Numerous studies correlate student literacy competence to performance in other content areas, post academic success, adult income levels, and a host of other measures. Research also provides school leaders with a roadmap for improving literacy instruction on their campus.

The author has observed that campuses making the most progress in the area of literacy performance often do so through a campus-wide focus in all content areas, not just English and reading courses. These observations have been in concert with the conclusions of Gina Biancarosa and Catherine Snow in their report, *Reading Next*. In the report, they summarize the elements of effective literacy programs. Their recommended elements are:

> *"direct, explicit comprehension instruction; effective instructional principles embedded in content; motivation and self-directed learning; text-based collaborative learning; strategic tutoring; diverse*

> *texts; intensive writing; a technology component; ongoing formative assessment of students; extended time for literacy; professional development; ongoing summative assessment of students and programs; teacher teams; leadership; and a comprehensive and coordinated literacy program."*

They further point out that though successful programs do not have to contain all of the elements, each successful program that they found did contain the following three elements: professional development, formative assessment, and summative assessment (2004, p. 4-5). These three critical elements can each be supported through the use of jump-start objectives.

Pay attention to reading and literacy performance and more students will gain competence in the one skill that may have the greatest impact on their academic and career success. Ignore literacy performance and possibly risk the future of all but the most resilient and self-motivated students.

Objective #22: Literacy

Our school will increase library circulation.

Objective Target:	At least a 20 percent increase in circulation should be selected.
Measurement Cycle:	Select three weeks, six weeks, or nine weeks.
Campus Levels:	This objective is appropriate for campuses serving any grade level.
Why:	The increased support of both academic and recreational reading should be the primary mission of any school library.
Power:	Central to the tenets of quality reading instruction is the need to ensure that students actually read more.
Implementation:	An easy way to achieve this objective is to extend library hours and increase student access to the library during the year.

Jump-start Objective - Planning and Tracking Tool

Jump-start Objective: *Our school will increase library circulation.*

Target: _____

Initial Data: _____

Measurement Cycle: _____

Initial Improvement Action(s)

- Action 1:_____
- Action 2:_____
- Action 3:_____

1st Check Point (____ / ____ / ____)

- Check Point Results:_____
- Revised Action(s): _____

2nd Check Point (____ / ____ / ____)

- Check Point Results:_____
- Revised Action(s): _____

3rd Check Point (____ / ____ / ____)

- Check Point Results:_____
- Revised Action(s): _____

4th Check Point (____ / ____ / ____)

- **Check Point Results:** _____
- **Revised Action(s):** _____

5th Check Point (____ / ____ / ____)

- **Check Point Results:** _____
- **Revised Action(s):** _____

6th Check Point (____ / ____ / ____)

- **Check Point Results:** _____
- **Revised Action(s):** _____

Responsible Parties:

_____
_____
_____
_____
_____
_____

Objective #23: Literacy

Our school will increase the number of books that students read in the Accelerated Reader program.

Accelerated Reader: *Accelerated Reader is a guided reading intervention that involves student reading of selected books, teacher monitoring, and short quizzes. For more information, visit www.renlearn.com/ar.*

Objective Target: At least a 20 percent increase in the number of books read should be selected.

Measurement Cycle: Select three weeks, four weeks, or six weeks.

Campus Levels: This objective is appropriate for campuses serving any grade level.

Why: Increasing the number of words that a student reads is directly correlated to increasing student reading ability (Allington, 2002).

Power:	Increased student reading performance is correlated to increased student academic performance in core instructional areas (Parker, Louie, & O'Dwyer, 2009).
Implementation:	An easy way to achieve this objective is to create individual, class, and grade level incentives and contests.

JUMP START YOUR SCHOOL!

Jump-start Objective - Planning and Tracking Tool

Jump-start Objective: *Our school will increase the number of books that students read in the Accelerated Reader program.*

Target: _____

Initial Data: _____

Measurement Cycle: _____

Initial Improvement Action(s)

- **Action 1:** _____
- **Action 2:** _____
- **Action 3:** _____

1st Check Point (____ / ____ / ____)

- **Check Point Results:** _____
- **Revised Action(s):** _____

2nd Check Point (____ / ____ / ____)

- **Check Point Results:** _____
- **Revised Action(s):** _____

3rd Check Point (___ / ___ / ___)

- **Check Point Results:**_____
- **Revised Action(s):** _____

4th Check Point (___ / ___ / ___)

- **Check Point Results:**_____
- **Revised Action(s):** _____

5th Check Point (___ / ___ / ___)

- **Check Point Results:**_____
- **Revised Action(s):** _____

6th Check Point (___ / ___ / ___)

- **Check Point Results:**_____
- **Revised Action(s):** _____

Responsible Parties:

_____
_____
_____
_____
_____
_____

Objective #24:   Literacy

Our school will increase the Lexile scores of our students.

Lexile: — *Lexile is a reading instrument that measures both reader ability and text difficulty on the same scale. Lexile scores are often considered more accurate than measures based on grade level. For more information, visit www.lexile.com.*

Objective Target: — At least a 100 point gain in Lexile scores for each thirty days should be selected.

Measurement Cycle: — Select three weeks, four weeks, or six weeks.

Campus Levels: — This objective is appropriate for campuses serving any grade level.

Why: — Increased student reading performance is correlated to increased student performance in core instructional areas (Parker, Louie, & O'Dwyer, 2009).

Power:	Focusing on Lexile scores can create accountability for reading improvement with all students, regardless of their current ability.
Implementation:	An easy way to achieve this objective is to embed a significant reading component in each course.

Jump-start Objective - Planning and Tracking Tool

Jump-start Objective: *Our school will increase the Lexile scores of our students.*

Target: _____

Initial Data: _____

Measurement Cycle: _____

Initial Improvement Action(s)

- Action 1:_____
- Action 2:_____
- Action 3:_____

1st Check Point (____ / ____ / ____)

- Check Point Results:_____
- Revised Action(s): _____

2nd Check Point (____ / ____ / ____)

- Check Point Results:_____
- Revised Action(s): _____

3rd Check Point (____ / ____ / ____)

- Check Point Results:_____
- Revised Action(s): _____

4ᵗʰ Check Point (____ / ____ / ____)

- **Check Point Results:** _____

- **Revised Action(s):** _____

5ᵗʰ Check Point (____ / ____ / ____)

- **Check Point Results:** _____

- **Revised Action(s):** _____

6ᵗʰ Check Point (____ / ____ / ____)

- **Check Point Results:** _____

- **Revised Action(s):** _____

Responsible Parties:

_____
_____
_____
_____
_____
_____

Objective #25: Literacy

Our school will increase student reading performance, as measured by pre and post assessments.

Objective Target:	On the post assessment, 70 percent of students will show growth of at least 5 percent.*
	* *The lowest recommended target.*
Measurement Cycle:	Select three weeks, six weeks, or nine weeks.
Campus Levels:	This objective is appropriate for campuses serving any grade level.
Why:	Increased student reading performance is correlated to increased student performance in core instructional areas (Parker, Louie, & O'Dwyer, 2009).
Power:	Reading ability is highly correlated to adult earning potential (Wright & Stenner, 1999).
Implementation:	An easy way to achieve this objective is to embed a significant reading component in each course.

Jump-start Objective - Planning and Tracking Tool

Jump-start Objective: *Our school will increase student reading performance, as measured by pre and post assessments.*

Target: _____

Initial Data: _____

Measurement Cycle: _____

Initial Improvement Action(s)

- Action 1:_____
- Action 2:_____
- Action 3:_____

1st Check Point (____ / ____ / ____)

- Check Point Results:_____
- Revised Action(s): _____

2nd Check Point (____ / ____ / ____)

- Check Point Results:_____
- Revised Action(s): _____

JUMP START YOUR SCHOOL!

3rd Check Point (____ / ____ / ____)

- **Check Point Results:**_____
- **Revised Action(s):** _____

4th Check Point (____ / ____ / ____)

- **Check Point Results:**_____
- **Revised Action(s):** _____

5th Check Point (____ / ____ / ____)

- **Check Point Results:**_____
- **Revised Action(s):** _____

6th Check Point (____ / ____ / ____)

- **Check Point Results:**_____
- **Revised Action(s):** _____

Responsible Parties:

_____
_____
_____
_____
_____
_____

Chapter 5: Grades and Grading

As student performance accountability increases, regardless if it is internal or external to the campus, an interesting anomaly often comes to light. The anomaly is the gap between classroom grades and performance on the accountability test or tests. A logical, yet often uncomfortable explanation for this gap exists. It generally occurs due to conflicting expectations. An individual teacher has one set of curricular expectations; the campus, district, state, and/or country have other sets of expectations. Throughout the year, teachers instruct and assign grades based on their expectations. However, at some point, the expectations of the larger entity are assessed, and because these can differ from those of the teacher, there is a discrepancy. Unfortunately for students, as the gaps between classroom, state, and national standards continue to increase, they bear the brunt of the consequences.

At the high school level, this difference between classroom and external accountability expectations manifests in dropout rates. In an *Education Week* article, Dean R. Lilliard, co-author of a national study on graduation rates with Phillip P. DeCicca, is quoted as saying, "We've gone to all these different data sources, and we consistently find a statistical relationship between the dropout rate and the graduation requirements. It's sort of like a wake- up call, we hope, to the research community to say, 'We need to pay attention to this,'" (Olson, 2000).

So who is at fault? Everyone shares some of the responsibility. However, to improve this situation, the lion's share of the work must occur at the classroom teacher and campus administrator level. Students and their families are best served when classroom expectations are aligned with those of the larger entities and when grades reflect progress and competency based on those shared expectations.

When large numbers of students can pass the class, but cannot pass the state test, the problem is best solved in the classroom. The commitment to increasing the correlation between classroom grades and larger accountability expectations not only provides students, teachers, and schools with useful data, but also sets the stage to make instruction more purposeful and students more competitive.

Objective #26: Grades and Grading

Our school will correlate course grading expectations and requirements to district and state testing standards in all core subjects.

Objective Target:	The targeted level of correlation should be at least 70 percent. This will mean that at least 70 percent of the students will have grades that are similar to their district and/or state test scores.
Measurement Cycle:	Select six weeks, nine weeks, or a semester.
Campus Levels:	This objective is appropriate for campuses serving any grade level.
Why:	In an aligned instructional system, course grades should be leading indicators of performance on common tests. A lack of correlation calls into question both the content and rigor of the course.
Power:	The author has observed that as campus expectations begin to match external expectations, instruction generally begins to improve and student success increases.

Implementation: This objective can be implemented through the purposeful and ongoing collaboration of teams of teachers.

Jump-start Objective - Planning and Tracking Tool

Jump-start Objective: *Our school will correlate course grading expectations and requirements to district and state testing standards in all core subjects.*

Target: _____

Initial Data: _____

Measurement Cycle: _____

Initial Improvement Action(s)

- **Action 1:** _____
- **Action 2:** _____
- **Action 3:** _____

1st Check Point (____ / ____ / ____)

- **Check Point Results:** _____
- **Revised Action(s):** _____

2nd Check Point (____ / ____ / ____)

- **Check Point Results:** _____
- **Revised Action(s):** _____

JUMP START YOUR SCHOOL!

3rd Check Point (_____ / _____ / _____)

- **Check Point Results:**_____
- **Revised Action(s):** _____

4th Check Point (_____ / _____ / _____)

- **Check Point Results:**_____
- **Revised Action(s):** _____

5th Check Point (_____ / _____ / _____)

- **Check Point Results:**_____
- **Revised Action(s):** _____

6th Check Point (_____ / _____ / _____)

- **Check Point Results:**_____
- **Revised Action(s):** _____

Responsible Parties:

_____
_____
_____
_____
_____
_____

Objective #27: Grades and Grading

Our school will increase the use of common grading rubrics in all core subject areas.

Objective Target:	At least a 30 percent increase in the usage of grading rubrics should be selected.
Measurement Cycle:	Select three weeks, six weeks, or nine weeks.
Campus Levels:	This objective is appropriate for campuses serving any grade level.
Why:	When there is increased understanding of assignment expectations by both teachers and students, the quality of both instruction and the resulting product generally improves (Lazear, 1998).
Power:	As the quality of instruction and student work increases, improved student and campus performance is generally the result.

Implementation: This objective is best implemented through the purposeful and ongoing collaboration of teams of teachers.

Jump-start Objective - Planning and Tracking Tool

Jump-start Objective: *Our school will increase the use of common grading rubrics in all core subject areas.*

Target: _____

Initial Data: _____

Measurement Cycle: _____

Initial Improvement Action(s)

- Action 1:_____
- Action 2:_____
- Action 3:_____

1ˢᵗ Check Point (____ / ____ / ____)

- Check Point Results:_____
- Revised Action(s): _____

2ⁿᵈ Check Point (____ / ____ / ____)

- Check Point Results:_____
- Revised Action(s): _____

3rd **Check Point** (____ / ____ / ____)

- **Check Point Results:**_____
- **Revised Action(s):** _____

4th **Check Point** (____ / ____ / ____)

- **Check Point Results:**_____
- **Revised Action(s):** _____

5th **Check Point** (____ / ____ / ____)

- **Check Point Results:**_____
- **Revised Action(s):** _____

6th **Check Point** (____ / ____ / ____)

- **Check Point Results:**_____
- **Revised Action(s):** _____

Responsible Parties:

_____

_____

_____

_____

_____

_____

Objective #28: Grades and Grading

Our school will increase the use of short-term, common assessments in all core courses.

Objective Target:	At least a 30 percent increase in the usage of common assessments should be selected.
Measurement Cycle:	Select two weeks, three weeks, four weeks, or six weeks.
Campus Levels:	This objective is appropriate for campuses serving any grade level.
Why:	The use of short-term common assessments provides teachers timely and relevant information on the content students have mastered and the content that must be reviewed or re-taught.

Power:	The author has observed that the use of short-term common assessments has two powerful benefits. First, the assessments assure that the campus/district curriculum is actually being taught. Second, it allows teacher teams to determine quickly which instructional strategies and practices have the most powerful and lasting impact on students.
Implementation:	This objective is easily implemented when the assessments are written and correlated by curriculum experts and provided to teachers.

Jump-start Objective - Planning and Tracking Tool

Jump-start Objective: *Our school will increase the use of short-term, common assessments in all core courses.*

Target: _____

Initial Data: _____

Measurement Cycle: _____

Initial Improvement Action(s)

- Action 1: _____
- Action 2: _____
- Action 3: _____

1st Check Point (____ / ____ / ____)

- Check Point Results: _____
- Revised Action(s): _____

2nd Check Point (____ / ____ / ____)

- Check Point Results: _____
- Revised Action(s): _____

JUMP START YOUR SCHOOL!

3rd Check Point (____ / ____ / ____)

- **Check Point Results:**_____
- **Revised Action(s):** _____

4th Check Point (____ / ____ / ____)

- **Check Point Results:**_____
- **Revised Action(s):** _____

5th Check Point (____ / ____ / ____)

- **Check Point Results:**_____
- **Revised Action(s):** _____

6th Check Point (____ / ____ / ____)

- **Check Point Results:**_____
- **Revised Action(s):** _____

Responsible Parties:

_____
_____
_____
_____
_____
_____

Objective #29: Grades and Grading

Our school will increase the use of mandatory, comprehensive, and common semester exams in all core courses.

Objective Target:	At least a 30 percent increase in the usage of mandatory, comprehensive, and common semester exams should be selected.
Measurement Cycle:	Select semester.
Campus Levels:	This objective is appropriate for secondary campuses.
Why:	The use of comprehensive semester exams can provide teachers and administrators with immediate and relevant data on the overall effectiveness of instruction.
Power:	As the overall effectiveness of instruction improves, so does student performance (Schmoker, 2006).
Implementation:	This objective is easily implemented when the exams are written and correlated by curriculum experts and provided to teachers.

Jump-start Objective - Planning and Tracking Tool

Jump-start Objective: *Our school will increase the use of mandatory, comprehensive, and common semester exams in all core courses.*

Target: _____

Initial Data: _____

Measurement Cycle: _____

Initial Improvement Action(s)

- Action 1:_____
- Action 2:_____
- Action 3:_____

1ˢᵗ Check Point (____ / ____ / ____)

- Check Point Results:_____
- Revised Action(s): _____

2ⁿᵈ Check Point (____ / ____ / ____)

- Check Point Results:_____
- Revised Action(s): _____

3rd Check Point (____ / ____ / ____)

- **Check Point Results:**_____
- **Revised Action(s):** _____

4th Check Point (____ / ____ / ____)

- **Check Point Results:**_____
- **Revised Action(s):** _____

5th Check Point (____ / ____ / ____)

- **Check Point Results:**_____
- **Revised Action(s):** _____

6th Check Point (____ / ____ / ____)

- **Check Point Results:**_____
- **Revised Action(s):** _____

Responsible Parties:

_____
_____
_____
_____
_____
_____

Objective #30: Grades and Grading

Our school will increase the percentage of students who pass all of their courses attempted in a given grading period.

Objective Target:	At least a 10 percent increase in the passing rate should be selected.
Measurement Cycle:	Select three weeks, six weeks, or nine weeks. The selected cycle should correlate with either the progress report schedule or the report card schedule.
Campus Levels:	This objective is appropriate for campuses serving any grade level.
Why:	The author has observed that increased student success lends itself to both increased student self-esteem and campus morale.
Power:	It has been observed that as students and teachers experience more success, the campus community as a whole begins to work harder to reach even higher levels of success.

Implementation: This objective is easily implemented through the use of goal setting, teacher support, tutoring, and student mentoring.

Jump-start Objective - Planning and Tracking Tool

Jump-start Objective: *Our school will increase the percentage of students who pass all of their courses attempted in a given grading period.*

Target: _____

Initial Data: _____

Measurement Cycle: _____

Initial Improvement Action(s)

- Action 1: _____
- Action 2: _____
- Action 3: _____

1st Check Point (____ / ____ / ____)

- **Check Point Results:** _____
- **Revised Action(s):** _____

2nd Check Point (____ / ____ / ____)

- **Check Point Results:** _____
- **Revised Action(s):** _____

3rd Check Point (____ / ____ / ____)

- Check Point Results: _____
- Revised Action(s): _____

4th Check Point (____ / ____ / ____)

- Check Point Results: _____
- Revised Action(s): _____

5th Check Point (____ / ____ / ____)

- Check Point Results: _____
- Revised Action(s): _____

6th Check Point (____ / ____ / ____)

- Check Point Results: _____
- Revised Action(s): _____

Responsible Parties:

_____
_____
_____
_____
_____
_____

Objective #31: Grades and Grading

Our school will decrease the student course failure rate.

Objective Target:	At least a 20 percent decrease in the failure rate should be selected.
Measurement Cycle:	Select three weeks, six weeks, or nine weeks. The selected cycle should correlate with either the progress report schedule or the report card schedule.
Campus Levels:	This objective is appropriate for campuses serving any grade level.
Why:	The author has observed that decreased student failure lends itself to both increased student self-esteem and campus morale.
Power:	It has been observed that as students and teachers experience more success, the campus community as a whole begins to work harder to reach even higher levels of success.

Implementation:	This objective is easily implemented through the use of goal setting, teacher support, tutoring, and student mentoring.

Jump-start Objective - Planning and Tracking Tool

Jump-start Objective: *Our school will decrease the student course failure rate.*

Target: _____

Initial Data: _____

Measurement Cycle: _____

Initial Improvement Action(s)

- Action 1:_____
- Action 2:_____
- Action 3:_____

1st Check Point (____ / ____ / ____)

- Check Point Results:_____
- Revised Action(s): _____

2nd Check Point (____ / ____ / ____)

- Check Point Results:_____
- Revised Action(s): _____

3rd Check Point (____ / ____ / ____)

- Check Point Results:_____
- Revised Action(s): _____

4th Check Point (____ / ____ / ____)

- **Check Point Results:**_____
- **Revised Action(s):** _____

5th Check Point (____ / ____ / ____)

- **Check Point Results:**_____
- **Revised Action(s):** _____

6th Check Point (____ / ____ / ____)

- **Check Point Results:**_____
- **Revised Action(s):** _____

Responsible Parties:

_____
_____
_____
_____
_____
_____

Objective #32: Grades and Grading

Our school will increase the number of students that qualify for either the A or A/B honor roll.

Objective Target:	At least a 10 percent increase in honor roll students should be selected.
Measurement Cycle:	Select six weeks, nine weeks, or a semester.
Campus Levels:	This objective is appropriate for campuses serving any grade level.
Why:	The author has observed that increased student success lends itself to both increased student self-esteem and campus morale.
Power:	It has been observed that as students and teachers experience more success, the campus community as a whole begins to work harder to reach even higher levels of success.
Implementation:	This objective is easily implemented through the use of goal setting, teacher support, tutoring, and student mentoring.

Jump-start Objective - Planning and Tracking Tool

Jump-start Objective: *Our school will increase the number of students that qualify for either the A or A/B honor roll.*

Target: _____

Initial Data: _____

Measurement Cycle: _____

Initial Improvement Action(s)

- Action 1:_____
- Action 2:_____
- Action 3:_____

1st Check Point (____ / ____ / ____)

- Check Point Results:_____
- Revised Action(s): _____

2nd Check Point (____ / ____ / ____)

- Check Point Results:_____
- Revised Action(s): _____

JUMP START YOUR SCHOOL!

3rd Check Point (____ / ____ / ____)

- **Check Point Results:**_____
- **Revised Action(s):** _____

4th Check Point (____ / ____ / ____)

- **Check Point Results:**_____
- **Revised Action(s):** _____

5th Check Point (____ / ____ / ____)

- **Check Point Results:**_____
- **Revised Action(s):** _____

6th Check Point (____ / ____ / ____)

- **Check Point Results:**_____
- **Revised Action(s):** _____

Responsible Parties:

_____
_____
_____
_____
_____
_____

Objective #33: Grades and Grading

Our school will increase student performance on common assessments and tests.

Objective Target:	At least 83 percent of students should score an 80 percent or higher, on a given assessment.
Measurement Cycle:	Select two weeks, three weeks, four weeks, or six weeks.
Campus Levels:	This objective is appropriate for campuses serving any grade level.
Why:	The author has observed that increased student performance on short-term assessments often increases the likelihood of meeting and/or exceeding long-term performance goals.
Power:	In order to achieve this goal, teachers must analyze instructional data and make incremental adjustments to their daily instruction.

Implementation: This objective is easily implemented through team based data analysis and adjustments to instructional practices.

Jump-start Objective - Planning and Tracking Tool

Jump-start Objective: *Our school will increase student performance on common assessments and tests.*

Target: _____

Initial Data: _____

Measurement Cycle: _____

Initial Improvement Action(s)

- Action 1:_____
- Action 2:_____
- Action 3:_____

1st Check Point (____ / ____ / ____)

- Check Point Results:_____
- Revised Action(s): _____

2nd Check Point (____ / ____ / ____)

- Check Point Results:_____
- Revised Action(s): _____

JUMP START YOUR SCHOOL!

3rd Check Point (____ / ____ / ____)

- **Check Point Results:**_____
- **Revised Action(s):** _____

4th Check Point (____ / ____ / ____)

- **Check Point Results:**_____
- **Revised Action(s):** _____

5th Check Point (____ / ____ / ____)

- **Check Point Results:**_____
- **Revised Action(s):** _____

6th Check Point (____ / ____ / ____)

- **Check Point Results:**_____
- **Revised Action(s):** _____

Responsible Parties:

_____
_____
_____
_____
_____
_____

Chapter 6: Student Engagement

Student engagement is a short chapter and just one short-term objective is presented. This is not because student engagement is not critical, it is. Most educators agree that authentic student engagement, the state where a student is intrinsically motivated to learn the content to further his or her own knowledge, is a critical component to improved student performance. The issue, as far as it relates to this book, is that the determination of authentic student engagement by observers is a subjective measure. Dr. Phillip Schlechty, in his 2005 book, *Creating Great Schools,* argues that authentic simply means what is real to the student. What an adult may view as part of his or her reality, such as the need to do an assignment and earn a good grade, may have no bearing on the reality of the student. The student's reality may be to not stand out in the classroom. Thus, a student's attention to an academic task could just as easily be a survival strategy, as it could be a strategy to acquire knowledge.

Countering the theoretical argument that authentic student engagement is difficult to determine, there are a number of campus leaders who have adopted the practice of instructional hyper-monitoring, who claim that after hundreds of classroom observations each year, they can recognize the difference between authentic engagement and compliant behavior. In other words, they believe that that they can tell the difference between a student doing a task because he or she wants to, versus because he or she has to. Based on the author's belief that there is an art and science to instructional pedagogy, the claims of the hyper-monitoring school leaders most likely have some validity.

For campuses that are making substantial progress in the areas of improving instructional rigor, relevance, and teacher pedagogy, looking at student engagement can be a logical next step. In a 2009 review of data from over 17,000 classroom observations, the author noted that as the bulk of student engagement shifts towards levels that are more authentic, on-task behavior increases, student discipline improves, and student performance begins to improve. At the very least, the pursuit of increasing student engagement should lend itself to the creating of a more student-centered learning environment.

Objective #34: Student Engagement

Our school will increase authentic student engagement on instructional tasks.

Objective Target:	A shift in student engagement from off task towards authentic of 4 percent to 8 percent, per measurement cycle, should be selected.
Measurement Cycle:	Select two weeks, three weeks, four weeks, or six weeks.
Campus Levels:	This objective is appropriate for campuses serving any grade level.
Why:	As students become more authentically engaged, retention and performance seems to improve.
Power:	As engagement increases, student discipline issues generally decrease.
Implementation:	This objective can be implemented through instruction at the application level and higher, and increased small group and collaborative activities.

Jump-start Objective - Planning and Tracking Tool

Jump-start Objective: *Our school will increase authentic student engagement on instructional tasks.*

Target: _____

Initial Data: _____

Measurement Cycle: _____

Initial Improvement Action(s)

- Action 1:_____
- Action 2:_____
- Action 3:_____

1st Check Point (____ / ____ / ____)

- **Check Point Results:**_____
- **Revised Action(s):** _____

2nd Check Point (____ / ____ / ____)

- **Check Point Results:**_____
- **Revised Action(s):** _____

3rd Check Point (____ / ____ / ____)

- **Check Point Results:**_____
- **Revised Action(s):** _____

4th Check Point (____ / ____ / ____)

- **Check Point Results:**_____
- **Revised Action(s):** _____

5th Check Point (____ / ____ / ____)

- **Check Point Results:**_____
- **Revised Action(s):** _____

6th Check Point (____ / ____ / ____)

- **Check Point Results:**_____
- **Revised Action(s):** _____

Responsible Parties:

_____
_____
_____
_____
_____
_____

Chapter 7: Special Needs Students

As passionately illustrated by Dr. Willard Daggett in a number of his recent presentations to educators, one characteristic of campuses that dramatically outperform their peers is the unwavering attention they pay to the needs of their most academically fragile students. These great campuses gain their sense of urgency and instructional insight by truly holding themselves accountable for the success of all their students.

Leadership and staffs of these campuses seem to understand that special needs students often are the canaries in the coalmine. They view the struggles and failures of academically fragile students as a reflection of the weaknesses of both campus systems and pedagogy. And in doing so, as they identify strategies and interventions that allow special needs students to succeed, they work to ensure that these practices are disseminated and used in every classroom, to the benefit of every student.

In the past, when miners noticed that the canary was struggling to breath, they did not blame the canary or label the canary as weak. Instead, the miners got out of the mine, changed the environment and immediately reassessed what they were doing. The analogy lends itself to schools. Pay attention to the most fragile students. The first noticeable symptom that instructional systems are unhealthy is when groups of academically fragile students begin to suffer and struggle for success. At that point, it is the responsibility of leadership, administrators, and pro-active teachers to change the instructional practices of the campus aggressively.

The objectives in this section are just a few examples of ways to focus on special needs students that will drive changes in pedagogy, consequently benefiting all students.

Objective #35: Special Needs

Our school will increase the number of special needs students served in the regular education setting.

Objective Target: At least a 20 percent increase in the number of special needs students served in regular education classrooms should be selected.

Measurement Cycle: Select four weeks, six weeks, or nine weeks.

Campus Levels: This objective is appropriate for campuses serving any grade level.

Why: It must be the practice of every campus to provide each student with the least restrictive educational environment. Not only is this the right thing to do, it is the law.

Power: The author has observed that the focus on the success of special needs students can drive improvement for the entire campus.

Implementation: One way to achieve this objective is to embed special education support in the regular classroom.

Jump-start Objective - Planning and Tracking Tool

Jump-start Objective: *Our school will increase the number of special needs students served in the regular education setting.*

Target: _____

Initial Data: _____

Measurement Cycle: _____

Initial Improvement Action(s)

- Action 1:_____
- Action 2:_____
- Action 3:_____

1ˢᵗ Check Point (____ / ____ / ____)

- Check Point Results:_____
- Revised Action(s): _____

2ⁿᵈ Check Point (____ / ____ / ____)

- Check Point Results:_____
- Revised Action(s): _____

3rd **Check Point** (____ / ____ / ____)

- **Check Point Results:** _____
- **Revised Action(s):** _____

4th **Check Point** (____ / ____ / ____)

- **Check Point Results:** _____
- **Revised Action(s):** _____

5th **Check Point** (____ / ____ / ____)

- **Check Point Results:** _____
- **Revised Action(s):** _____

6th **Check Point** (____ / ____ / ____)

- **Check Point Results:** _____
- **Revised Action(s):** _____

Responsible Parties:

_____
_____
_____
_____
_____
_____

Objective #36: Special Needs

Our school will increase the number of special education inclusion students that pass their courses with at least 75 percent proficiency.

Objective Target:	At least a 25 percent increase in the number of students scoring at or above 75 percent proficiency should be selected.
Measurement Cycle:	Select two weeks, three weeks, four weeks, six weeks, or nine weeks.
Campus Levels:	This objective is appropriate for campuses serving any grade level.
Why:	The more success a student has in his or her classes, the more likely he or she will remain enrolled in school (Human Resources and Skill Development Canada, 2000).

Power:	The instructional strategies and practices that allow special education students to survive in the classroom can also increase the performance of other students in the class.
Implementation:	One way to achieve this objective is to ensure that every teacher has received training and support in instructional modifications.

Jump-start Objective - Planning and Tracking Tool

Jump-start Objective: *Our school will increase the number of special education inclusion students that pass their courses with at least 75 percent proficiency.*

Target: _____

Initial Data: _____

Measurement Cycle: _____

Initial Improvement Action(s)

- Action 1:_____
- Action 2:_____
- Action 3:_____

1st Check Point (____ / ____ / ____)

- Check Point Results:_____
- Revised Action(s): _____

2nd Check Point (____ / ____ / ____)

- Check Point Results:_____
- Revised Action(s): _____

3rd Check Point (____ / ____ / ____)

- **Check Point Results:**_____
- **Revised Action(s):** _____

4th Check Point (____ / ____ / ____)

- **Check Point Results:**_____
- **Revised Action(s):** _____

5th Check Point (____ / ____ / ____)

- **Check Point Results:**_____
- **Revised Action(s):** _____

6th Check Point (____ / ____ / ____)

- **Check Point Results:**_____
- **Revised Action(s):** _____

Responsible Parties:

_____
_____
_____
_____
_____
_____

Chapter 8: Communication Skills

Why should a campus focus on improving communication skills? There are a number of excellent reasons to do so. First, as Dr. Mike Schmoker discusses in *Results Now* (2006), the practice of taking sub-conscious thoughts and making them conscious through critical writing and discussions, creates meanings and connections for students. Second, most educators would agree that lots of authentic, academic talk is a sign of a healthy learning environment. Third, excellent communication skills are a quality that many employers look for when making hiring decisions. These are just a few of the reasons to focus on making students better communicators. The endeavor to teach students to articulate the concepts they are learning and to make this part of the day-to-day fabric of campus life is both worthwhile and powerful.

Unfortunately, based on numerous anecdotal observations by the author, many schools drop the ball when it comes to providing students the opportunity to practice their communication skills and become better communicators. They are fooled by appearances. They believe that because there are always some students purposely discussing academics, that all students must be doing so on a regular basis. This is not the case. Students that are inclined to engage in academic talk take advantage of the available opportunities. Those that are not inclined simply elect not to do so.

Therefore, the challenge to campuses is to create an environment and expectation that all students will be competent communicators and that each student will have numerous opportunities to practice his or her skills.

Objective #37: Communication Skills

Our students will create and present one oral report per semester, in each course.

Objective Target:	On the oral reports, at least 80 percent of students will score an 80 percent or higher, based on a pre-determined rubric.*
	* The lowest recommended target.
Measurement Cycle:	Select six weeks, nine weeks, or a semester.
Campus Levels:	This objective is appropriate for campuses serving any grade level.
Why:	Public speaking is a critical, real world skill that receives little attention and practice by the average student.
Power:	Presenting ideas and material verbally takes subconscious concepts and makes them conscious understandings (Schmoker, 2006).

Implementation: One way to achieve this objective is have teams of teachers select the concepts or topics to be covered and build the report rubric prior to the activity. Then as part of the overall lesson, students are given a template to use while developing their presentation.

Jump-start Objective - Planning and Tracking Tool

Jump-start Objective: *Our students will create and present one oral report per semester, in each course.*

Target: _____

Initial Data: _____

Measurement Cycle: _____

Initial Improvement Action(s)

- Action 1:_____
- Action 2:_____
- Action 3:_____

1st Check Point (____ / ____ / ____)

- Check Point Results:_____
- Revised Action(s): _____

2nd Check Point (____ / ____ / ____)

- Check Point Results:_____
- Revised Action(s): _____

3rd **Check Point** (____ / ____ / ____)

- **Check Point Results:**_____
- **Revised Action(s):** _____

4th **Check Point** (____ / ____ / ____)

- **Check Point Results:**_____
- **Revised Action(s):** _____

5th **Check Point** (____ / ____ / ____)

- **Check Point Results:**_____
- **Revised Action(s):** _____

6th **Check Point** (____ / ____ / ____)

- **Check Point Results:**_____
- **Revised Action(s):** _____

Responsible Parties:

_____
_____
_____
_____
_____
_____

Objective #38: Communication Skills

Our students will enroll in a speech course. Eighty percent of all students will receive a grade of 80 percent or above in the course.

Objective Target:	Eighty percent of students will earn a grade of 80 percent or above in the course.*
	* The lowest recommended target.
Measurement Cycle:	Select six weeks, nine weeks, or a semester.
Campus Levels:	This objective is appropriate for secondary campuses.
Why:	Public speaking is a critical, real world skill that receives little attention and practice by the average student.
Power:	The ability to make rational arguments and defend positions is a recognized as a critical, real world skill.

Implementation: Make the speech class a semester long course that can be paired with either a physical education, health, and/or an introductory technology course.

Jump-start Objective - Planning and Tracking Tool

Jump-start Objective: *Our students will enroll in a speech course. Eighty percent of all students will receive a grade of 80 percent or above in the course.*

Target: _____

Initial Data: _____

Measurement Cycle: _____

Initial Improvement Action(s)

- Action 1:_____
- Action 2:_____
- Action 3:_____

1st Check Point (____ / ____ / ____)

- Check Point Results:_____
- Revised Action(s): _____

2nd Check Point (____ / ____ / ____)

- Check Point Results:_____
- Revised Action(s): _____

3rd **Check Point** (____ / ____ / ____)

- **Check Point Results:**_____
- **Revised Action(s):** _____

4th **Check Point** (____ / ____ / ____)

- **Check Point Results:**_____
- **Revised Action(s):** _____

5th **Check Point** (____ / ____ / ____)

- **Check Point Results:**_____
- **Revised Action(s):** _____

6th **Check Point** (____ / ____ / ____)

- **Check Point Results:**_____
- **Revised Action(s):** _____

Responsible Parties:

_____
_____
_____
_____
_____
_____

Objective #39:   Communication Skills

Our school will increase the percentage of students who are able to articulate the learning objective of a given class, when asked.

Objective Target:	A 3 percentage point increase, each three weeks, in the number of students who can articulate the learning objective when asked.*
	The highest recommended target
Measurement Cycle:	Select three weeks or six weeks.
Campus Levels:	This objective is appropriate for campuses serving any grade level.
Why:	Students being able to explain what they are learning is one way for instructional staff to determine that the material being covered is actually being learned.
Power:	Being able to articulate the learning objective is a way for a student to connect information and concepts (Schmoker, 2006).

Implementation:	There are three simple steps to implementing this objective. First, make it a practice that teachers prominently display the learning objective for each class, each day. Second, make it a practice that teachers discuss the learning objective with each class during the introduction portion of the lesson. Third, when support staff visit classrooms they should ask students what they are learning today.

Jump-start Objective - Planning and Tracking Tool

Jump-start Objective: *Our school will increase the percentage of students who are able to articulate the learning objective of a given class, when asked.*

Target: _____

Initial Data: _____

Measurement Cycle: _____

Initial Improvement Action(s)

- **Action 1:**_____
- **Action 2:**_____
- **Action 3:**_____

1ˢᵗ **Check Point (** ____ / ____ / ____ **)**

- **Check Point Results:**_____
- **Revised Action(s):** _____

2ⁿᵈ **Check Point (** ____ / ____ / ____ **)**

- **Check Point Results:**_____
- **Revised Action(s):** _____

JUMP START YOUR SCHOOL!

3rd Check Point (____ / ____ / ____)

- **Check Point Results:**_____
- **Revised Action(s):** _____

4th Check Point (____ / ____ / ____)

- **Check Point Results:**_____
- **Revised Action(s):** _____

5th Check Point (____ / ____ / ____)

- **Check Point Results:**_____
- **Revised Action(s):** _____

6th Check Point (____ / ____ / ____)

- **Check Point Results:**_____
- **Revised Action(s):** _____

Responsible Parties:

_____
_____
_____
_____
_____
_____

Objective #40: Communication Skills

Our school will increase the number of students enrolled in either dual-language or foreign language classes.

Objective Target:	At least a 5 percent increase in enrollment should be selected.
Measurement Cycle:	Select semester.
Campus Levels:	This objective is appropriate for campuses serving any grade level.
Why:	The ability to converse in a second language is a critical, marketable, real world skill that receives little attention and practice by the average student.
Power:	Students who study a foreign language have been shown to outperform their peers who are only enrolled in English courses (Carr, 1994).

Implementation: This objective can be implemented through recruiting students and an emphasis by campus leadership on the importance of becoming bilingual.

Jump-start Objective - Planning and Tracking Tool

Jump-start Objective: *Our school will increase the number of students enrolled in either dual-language or foreign language classes.*

Target: _____

Initial Data: _____

Measurement Cycle: _____

Initial Improvement Action(s)

- Action 1:_____
- Action 2:_____
- Action 3:_____

1st Check Point (____ / ____ / ____)

- Check Point Results:_____
- Revised Action(s): _____

2nd Check Point (____ / ____ / ____)

- Check Point Results:_____
- Revised Action(s): _____

JUMP START YOUR SCHOOL!

3rd Check Point (____ / ____ / ____)

- **Check Point Results:**_____
- **Revised Action(s):** _____

4th Check Point (____ / ____ / ____)

- **Check Point Results:**_____
- **Revised Action(s):** _____

5th Check Point (____ / ____ / ____)

- **Check Point Results:**_____
- **Revised Action(s):** _____

6th Check Point (____ / ____ / ____)

- **Check Point Results:**_____
- **Revised Action(s):** _____

Responsible Parties:

_____

_____

_____

_____

_____

_____

Chapter 9: School Clubs, Co-curricular and Extracurricular Activities, and Community Service

When one analyzes the enrollment of alternative campuses, especially discipline programs, it quickly becomes evident that, for the most part, the enrolled students are the ones that are generally the least connected to the regular school. These students typically are not in the arts, academic clubs, or on the athletic teams.

The more connected a student is to school and the school community, the more likely it is the student will be academically successful and graduate (O'Brien & Rollefson, 1995). Therefore, a school leader has a compelling reason to pay attention to participation rates in campus clubs, teams, and organizations.

Many educators believe it is in the best interest of both students and the school to increase enrollment and participation in school clubs, co-curricular and extracurricular activities, and community service. However, achieving this is not quite as easy as it would seem. Often a critical first obstacle to address is the sponsors. These same sponsors, that without question, are more than willing to teach, mentor, and/or coach any student that shows up, often are not comfortable recruiting students. However, increasing enrollment and participation is more than just the act of "opening the door." Many students need to be led through the door. As such, active recruiting is a must.

Most students are searching for a sense of belonging and purpose. They have an innate need to find something to fill their time and bring meaning and reward to their day. Average schools accept whatever their students are inclined to do. Great schools do not leave this to chance; they steer their students into, and then keep them involved in, healthy, purposeful activities.

What are you willing to accept?

Objective #41: School Clubs, Co-curricular and Extracurricular Activities, and Community Service

Our school will increase the number of students who currently participate in campus clubs, co-curricular and/or extracurricular activities.

Objective Target:	At least a 10 percent increase in student participation should be selected.
Measurement Cycle:	Select six weeks, nine weeks, twelve weeks, or a semester.
Campus Levels:	This objective is appropriate for campuses serving any grade level.
Why:	Research shows that the more vested students are in the school community, the more successful they are (O'Brien & Rollefson, 1995).

Power:	Students actively involved in campus clubs, co-curricular, and extracurricular activities have fewer discipline problems, earn higher grades, and have a lower dropout rate than their peers that do not participate (O'Brien & Rollefson).
Implementation:	An easy way to achieve this objective is to cast campus sponsors and coaches as recruiters. Instead of passively accepting any student that chooses to be a part of their activity, sponsors and coaches should be expected to actively recruit and retain students in their clubs, organizations, and teams.

Jump-start Objective - Planning and Tracking Tool

Jump-start Objective: *Our school will increase the number of students who currently participate in campus clubs, co-curricular and/or extracurricular activities.*

Target: _____

Initial Data: _____

Measurement Cycle: _____

Initial Improvement Action(s)

- Action 1:_____
- Action 2:_____
- Action 3:_____

1st Check Point (____ / ____ / ____)

- Check Point Results:_____
- Revised Action(s): _____

2nd Check Point (____ / ____ / ____)

- Check Point Results:_____
- Revised Action(s): _____

JUMP START YOUR SCHOOL!

3rd Check Point (____ / ____ / ____)

- **Check Point Results:**_____
- **Revised Action(s):** _____

4th Check Point (____ / ____ / ____)

- **Check Point Results:**_____
- **Revised Action(s):** _____

5th Check Point (____ / ____ / ____)

- **Check Point Results:**_____
- **Revised Action(s):** _____

6th Check Point (____ / ____ / ____)

- **Check Point Results:**_____
- **Revised Action(s):** _____

Responsible Parties:

_____

_____

_____

_____

_____

_____

Objective #42: School Clubs, Co-curricular and Extracurricular Activities, and Community Service

Our students will visit (select number) cultural museum(s). Each student will produce a written reflection of his or her learning while on the visit.

    Objective Target: On the written reflection, 80 percent of students will score 80 percent or higher, based on a pre-determined rubric.*

    The lowest recommended target.

    Measurement Cycle: Select six weeks, nine weeks, twelve weeks, or a semester.

    Campus Levels: This objective is appropriate for campuses serving any grade level.

    Why: Many educators see the value of extending learning beyond the classroom.

Power:	By expecting a student product, the campus ensures that field trips become purposeful academic activities.
Implementation:	One way to achieve this objective is have teams of teachers select the activity and build the written reflection rubric prior to the field trip. Before the trip, students should discuss the activity in class and be given a template to use while at the site to take notes and make observations.

Jump-start Objective - Planning and Tracking Tool

Jump-start Objective: *Our students will visit _____ cultural museum(s). Each student will produce a written reflection of his or her learning while on the visit.*

Target: _____

Initial Data: _____

Measurement Cycle: _____

Initial Improvement Action(s)

- Action 1: _____
- Action 2: _____
- Action 3: _____

1st Check Point (____ / ____ / ____)

- Check Point Results: _____
- Revised Action(s): _____

2nd Check Point (____ / ____ / ____)

- Check Point Results: _____
- Revised Action(s): _____

3rd **Check Point** (____ / ____ / ____)

- **Check Point Results:**_____
- **Revised Action(s):** _____

4th **Check Point** (____ / ____ / ____)

- **Check Point Results:**_____
- **Revised Action(s):** _____

5th **Check Point** (____ / ____ / ____)

- **Check Point Results:**_____
- **Revised Action(s):** _____

6th **Check Point** (____ / ____ / ____)

- **Check Point Results:**_____
- **Revised Action(s):** _____

Responsible Parties:

_____

_____

_____

_____

_____

_____

Objective #43: School Clubs, Co-curricular and Extracurricular Activities, and Community Service

Our school will increase the percentage of students that participate in at least two campus sanctioned community service or service learning projects.

Objective Target:	Select a target that represents at least a 10 percent increase in student participation.
Measurement Cycle:	Select three weeks, six weeks, twelve weeks, or a semester.
Campus Levels:	This objective is appropriate for campuses serving any grade level.
Why:	Community service and service learning activities are ways to add real world relevance to instruction.

Power: The author has observed that the success, positive feedback, and esprit de corp that result from participating in community service and service learning activities can quickly become a source of student self-esteem and campus pride.

Implementation: First, start small and local. Look for ways to work on campus. A community vegetable garden is one example. Second, embed a project in each core subject. A garden could be the science project. A food drive could be the math project. Third, as a requirement for membership or participation, have each team, club, and group complete at least one project each year.

Jump-start Objective - Planning and Tracking Tool

Jump-start Objective: *Our school will increase the percentage of students that participate in at least two campus sanctioned community service or service learning projects.*

Target: _____

Initial Data: _____

Measurement Cycle: _____

Initial Improvement Action(s)

- Action 1:_____
- Action 2:_____
- Action 3:_____

1ˢᵗ Check Point (____ / ____ / ____)

- Check Point Results:_____
- Revised Action(s): _____

2ⁿᵈ Check Point (____ / ____ / ____)

- Check Point Results:_____
- Revised Action(s): _____

JUMP START YOUR SCHOOL!

3rd Check Point (____ / ____ / ____)

- **Check Point Results:**_____
- **Revised Action(s):** _____

4th Check Point (____ / ____ / ____)

- **Check Point Results:**_____
- **Revised Action(s):** _____

5th Check Point (____ / ____ / ____)

- **Check Point Results:**_____
- **Revised Action(s):** _____

6th Check Point (____ / ____ / ____)

- **Check Point Results:**_____
- **Revised Action(s):** _____

Responsible Parties:

_____
_____
_____
_____
_____
_____

Chapter 10: Technology

This chapter showcases only one sample objective. Though campuses that the author has worked with have developed numerous short-term objectives for technology, they are purposely not presented in this book. That is not to indicate that technology is not important, it is. However, technology is not the end all, and it is not a replacement for quality instruction. It is a tool, a resource to be implemented and manipulated effectively by teachers and students, but a tool nonetheless.

In terms of technology implementation and use, schools fall into four basic categories. The objectives that a campus uses should be based on the category in which the campus currently fits. Most campuses generally occupy either of the last two categories discussed in this chapter.

The first category is made up of schools that do not have adequate hardware, software, and/or connectivity. If a campus falls into this category, it is recommended that selected objectives center on rectifying this situation.

The second category is made up of campuses that have hardware, software, and connectivity, but have yet to build up a critical mass of staff who are competent and comfortable using technology in their classrooms. If a campus falls in this category, it is recommended that selected objectives focus on staff training and capacity building.

The third category is made up of campuses that have the infrastructure and trained staff, but the use of technology throughout the day by students and teachers is limited. If a campus falls into this category, it is recommended that selected objectives focus on increasing the use of the available equipment. The jump-start objective presented in this chapter is appropriate for a campus in this category.

The fourth category is made up of campuses that have infrastructure, trained staff, and regular and adequate use of technology in the classroom and by students. These campuses need to focus on the integration of technology into content areas with embedded, meaningful projects. The key is to ensure that an ever increasing number of students meet project quality standards.

Objective #44: Technology

Our school will increase student use of technology in the classroom.

Objective Target:	An observed increase in the student use of technology of 2 percent to 5 percent, per measurement cycle, should be selected.
Measurement Cycle:	Select three weeks, four weeks, six weeks, or nine weeks.
Campus Levels:	This objective is appropriate for campuses serving any grade level.
Why:	Many experts predict that students who are not technologically literate will have difficulty adapting to meet the requirements of many emerging careers.
Power:	The ability to use technology effectively is becoming more and more critical for career success.

Implementation: This objective can be implemented through professional development and increased team planning by teachers, and the assigning of specific projects.

Jump-start Objective - Planning and Tracking Tool

Jump-start Objective: *Our school will increase student use of technology in the classroom.*

Target: _____

Initial Data: _____

Measurement Cycle: _____

Initial Improvement Action(s)

- Action 1:_____
- Action 2:_____
- Action 3:_____

1ˢᵗ Check Point (____ / ____ / ____)

- Check Point Results:_____
- Revised Action(s): _____

2ⁿᵈ Check Point (____ / ____ / ____)

- Check Point Results:_____
- Revised Action(s): _____

JUMP START YOUR SCHOOL!

3rd Check Point (____ / ____ / ____)

    • **Check Point Results:**_____

    • **Revised Action(s):** _____

4th Check Point (____ / ____ / ____)

    • **Check Point Results:**_____

    • **Revised Action(s):** _____

5th Check Point (____ / ____ / ____)

    • **Check Point Results:**_____

    • **Revised Action(s):** _____

6th Check Point (____ / ____ / ____)

    • **Check Point Results:**_____

    • **Revised Action(s):** _____

Responsible Parties:

_____

_____

_____

_____

_____

_____

Chapter 11: Graduation and Beyond

Graduation, the driving goal of schools and what every educator desires for all of his or her students. Master the curriculum, pass your exams, and prepare yourself for success in the real world; that is message that is constantly preached to students. Remember though, teaching is just the means to the ends. It is the performance of students after they graduate that is the ultimate measure of the effectiveness of instruction.

Every student must be both willing and prepared to extend their learning after they leave high school. But preparing and encouraging students to further their education is not just the responsibility of the twelfth grade. Every campus, every grade level, and every teacher has a stake in the adult success of students. As such, it is entirely appropriate that schools at all levels have objectives that reflect this reality.

Objective #45:   Graduation and Beyond

Our students will be required to create and present a project based on their current college degree and/or career path of choice.

> Objective Target: Eighty percent of students will score 80 percent or higher on the project, based on a pre-determined rubric.*
>
> *The lowest recommended target.*
>
> Measurement Cycle: Select nine weeks, twelve weeks, or a semester.
>
> Campus Levels: This objective is appropriate for campuses serving any grade level.
>
> Why: Presenting plans and goals takes subconscious ideas and makes achieving them possible.
>
> Power: Research suggests that the parents of high socio-economic status students are more focused on college and more involved in the enrollment process than the parents of low socio-economic students. This objective is a powerful way for schools and teachers to begin to level the playing field for all students (Rowan-Kenyon, Bell, & Perna, 2008).

Implementation: One way to achieve this objective is to block out specific time in the calendar for the project and have teams of teachers build the project rubric prior to the activity.

Jump-start Objective - Planning and Tracking Tool

Jump-start Objective: *Our students will be required to create and present a project based on their current college degree and/or career path of choice.*

Target: _____

Initial Data: _____

Measurement Cycle: _____

Initial Improvement Action(s)

- Action 1: _____
- Action 2: _____
- Action 3: _____

1st Check Point (____ / ____ / ____)

- **Check Point Results:** _____
- **Revised Action(s):** _____

2nd Check Point (____ / ____ / ____)

- **Check Point Results:** _____
- **Revised Action(s):** _____

3rd Check Point (____ / ____ / ____)

- **Check Point Results:**_____
- **Revised Action(s):** _____

4th Check Point (____ / ____ / ____)

- **Check Point Results:**_____
- **Revised Action(s):** _____

5th Check Point (____ / ____ / ____)

- **Check Point Results:**_____
- **Revised Action(s):** _____

6th Check Point (____ / ____ / ____)

- **Check Point Results:**_____
- **Revised Action(s):** _____

Responsible Parties:

Objective #46: Graduation and Beyond

Our school will decrease the dropout rate.

Objective Target:	This target is dependent on the severity of the dropout problem. The greater the problem, the more aggressive the selected target should be. Choose between a 10 percent to 50 percent reduction in dropouts.
Measurement Cycle:	Select six weeks, nine weeks, or a semester.
Campus Levels:	This objective is appropriate for secondary campuses.
Why:	Significantly increasing the number of students who graduate is one of the most powerful tasks a school can accomplish.
Power:	Reducing the number of students who dropout changes lives, improves the community, and saves taxpayer dollars.

Implementation: This objective can be implemented through focusing on student needs, providing timely interventions, and improving student/staff relationships.

Jump-start Objective - Planning and Tracking Tool

Jump-start Objective: *Our school will decrease the dropout rate.*

Target: _____

Initial Data: _____

Measurement Cycle: _____

Initial Improvement Action(s)

- Action 1:_____
- Action 2:_____
- Action 3:_____

1st Check Point (____ / ____ / ____)

- Check Point Results:_____
- Revised Action(s): _____

2nd Check Point (____ / ____ / ____)

- Check Point Results:_____
- Revised Action(s): _____

3rd Check Point (____ / ____ / ____)

- Check Point Results:_____
- Revised Action(s): _____

4ᵗʰ Check Point (____ / ____ / ____)

- **Check Point Results:** _____
- **Revised Action(s):** _____

5ᵗʰ Check Point (____ / ____ / ____)

- **Check Point Results:** _____
- **Revised Action(s):** _____

6ᵗʰ Check Point (____ / ____ / ____)

- **Check Point Results:** _____
- **Revised Action(s):** _____

Responsible Parties:

_____
_____
_____
_____
_____
_____

Objective #47: Graduation and Beyond

Our school will increase the number of students that graduate in four years or less.

Objective Target:	This target is dependent on the severity of the extended-year graduation problem. The greater the problem, the more aggressive the selected target should be. Choose between a 20 percent to 50 percent reduction in extended-year graduates.
Measurement Cycle:	Select semester.
Campus Levels:	This objective is appropriate for secondary campuses.
Why:	A student's best chance to graduate occurs within the traditional four-year window.
Power:	Improving four-year graduation rates reduces the number of dropouts, reduces staffing needs, and saves taxpayer money.

Implementation: This objective can be implemented through the reduction of failure rates, improved scheduling, and timely student interventions.

Jump-start Objective - Planning and Tracking Tool

Jump-start Objective: *Our school will increase the number of students that graduate in four years or less.*

Target: _____

Initial Data: _____

Measurement Cycle: _____

Initial Improvement Action(s)

- Action 1:_____
- Action 2:_____
- Action 3:_____

1st Check Point (____ / ____ / ____)

- Check Point Results:_____
- Revised Action(s): _____

2nd Check Point (____ / ____ / ____)

- Check Point Results:_____
- Revised Action(s): _____

3rd Check Point (____ / ____ / ____)

- **Check Point Results:**_____
- **Revised Action(s):** _____

4th Check Point (____ / ____ / ____)

- **Check Point Results:**_____
- **Revised Action(s):** _____

5th Check Point (____ / ____ / ____)

- **Check Point Results:**_____
- **Revised Action(s):** _____

6th Check Point (____ / ____ / ____)

- **Check Point Results:**_____
- **Revised Action(s):** _____

Responsible Parties:

_____
_____
_____
_____
_____
_____

Objective #48: Graduation and Beyond

Our school will increase the percentage of graduates enrolling in college, technical schools, or the military.

Objective Target:	This target is dependent on the number of students not extending their education. The greater the number, the more aggressive the selected target should be. Choose between a 10 percent to 50 percent increase in enrollment.
Measurement Cycle:	Select semester.
Campus Levels:	This objective is appropriate for secondary campuses.
Why:	Increasing post-secondary enrollment increases the relevance of current courses and academic work.
Power:	Increasing the number of students continuing their education increases the overall chance of adult success for graduates.

Implementation: This objective can be implemented through the reduction of failure rates, the increase in four-year graduation rates, and aggressive mentoring.

Jump-start Objective - Planning and Tracking Tool

Jump-start Objective: *Our school will increase the percentage of graduates enrolling in college, technical schools, or the military.*

Target: _____

Initial Data: _____

Measurement Cycle: _____

Initial Improvement Action(s)

- Action 1:_____
- Action 2:_____
- Action 3:_____

1st Check Point (____ / ____ / ____)

- Check Point Results:_____
- Revised Action(s): _____

2nd Check Point (____ / ____ / ____)

- Check Point Results:_____
- Revised Action(s): _____

3rd **Check Point** (____ / ____ / ____)

- **Check Point Results:**_____
- **Revised Action(s):** _____

4th **Check Point** (____ / ____ / ____)

- **Check Point Results:**_____
- **Revised Action(s):** _____

5th **Check Point** (____ / ____ / ____)

- **Check Point Results:**_____
- **Revised Action(s):** _____

6th **Check Point** (____ / ____ / ____)

- **Check Point Results:**_____
- **Revised Action(s):** _____

Responsible Parties:

_____
_____
_____
_____
_____
_____

Objective #49:   Graduation and Beyond

Our school will decrease the number of students that require remedial courses during their first year of college.

Objective Target:	The selected target should represent at least a 10 percent decrease in the number of students needing remedial courses.
Measurement Cycle:	Select semester.
Campus Levels:	This objective is appropriate for secondary campuses.
Why:	Decreasing the need for college remediation increases the relevance of current courses and academic work.
Power:	Focusing on the needs of graduates provides an impetus for updating and aligning curriculum.
Implementation:	This objective can be implemented through updated curriculum, improved instructional practices, and systemic academic interventions.

Jump-start Objective - Planning and Tracking Tool

Jump-start Objective: *Our school will decrease the number of students that require remedial courses during their first year of college.*

Target: _____

Initial Data: _____

Measurement Cycle: _____

Initial Improvement Action(s)

- Action 1:_____
- Action 2:_____
- Action 3:_____

1ˢᵗ Check Point (____ / ____ / ____)

- Check Point Results:_____
- Revised Action(s): _____

2ⁿᵈ Check Point (____ / ____ / ____)

- Check Point Results:_____
- Revised Action(s): _____

3rd **Check Point** (____ / ____ / ____)

- **Check Point Results:**_____
- **Revised Action(s):** _____

4th **Check Point** (____ / ____ / ____)

- **Check Point Results:**_____
- **Revised Action(s):** _____

5th **Check Point** (____ / ____ / ____)

- **Check Point Results:**_____
- **Revised Action(s):** _____

6th **Check Point** (____ / ____ / ____)

- **Check Point Results:**_____
- **Revised Action(s):** _____

Responsible Parties:

_____
_____
_____
_____
_____
_____

Objective #50:   Graduation and Beyond

Our school will increase the overall amount of grants and scholarships awarded to graduates.

Objective Target:	Select at least a 25 percent increase in the number of students receiving awards. Some campuses have more than doubled the dollar amount of grants and scholarships received by students in just the first year of focusing on this objective.
Measurement Cycle:	Select semester.
Campus Levels:	This objective is appropriate for secondary campuses.
Why:	Providing guidance and support in securing post-secondary funding can facilitate the creation of a campus-wide college-going culture.
Power:	Securing adequate financial support is a critical component in increasing a student's chances of completing a post-secondary program.

Implementation: This objective can be implemented through increasing college enrollment, aggressive school counseling, and an overall campus focus on life-long learning and continuing education.

Jump-start Objective - Planning and Tracking Tool

Jump-start Objective: *Our school will increase the overall amount of grants and scholarships awarded to graduates.*

Target: _____

Initial Data: _____

Measurement Cycle: _____

Initial Improvement Action(s)

- Action 1: _____
- Action 2: _____
- Action 3: _____

1st Check Point (____ / ____ / ____)

- Check Point Results: _____
- Revised Action(s): _____

2nd Check Point (____ / ____ / ____)

- Check Point Results: _____
- Revised Action(s): _____

JUMP START YOUR SCHOOL!

3rd Check Point (____ / ____ / ____)

- **Check Point Results:** _____
- **Revised Action(s):** _____

4th Check Point (____ / ____ / ____)

- **Check Point Results:** _____
- **Revised Action(s):** _____

5th Check Point (____ / ____ / ____)

- **Check Point Results:** _____
- **Revised Action(s):** _____

6th Check Point (____ / ____ / ____)

- **Check Point Results:** _____
- **Revised Action(s):** _____

Responsible Parties:

_____
_____
_____
_____
_____
_____

Chapter 12: Rubrics

As a campus begins collecting short-term data from many of the objectives in this book, the staff will find that the adoption of project and grading rubrics will become more and more useful. The effective use of data is built on the ability to compare apples to apples. Campus leadership and teams of teachers will be able to better gauge improvement and identify promising practices when project requirements are determined prior to implementation and the definition of quality work is uniform, communicated, and understood by both adults and students.

Rubrics allow a campus to build a better understanding of what constitutes quality. This understanding then lends itself to both the development of more meaningful classroom assignments and increased student performance.

An excellent resource for developing rubrics is the Rubistar website. This free site, supported by the United States Department of Education, provides teachers with customizable rubric templates that can be used for any number of projects and assignments. The web address is www.rubistar.4teachers.org.

Chapter 13: Conclusion

Hopefully, this book has sparked your enthusiasm for using short-term objectives to improve school performance. Use these objectives to start immediately, but over time, as you gain insight and understanding, create your own.

When you visit great schools, you immediately notice that the staff seems extraordinarily smart. However, they really are not smarter than everyone else. What they have been able to do is successfully deal with the issues that confound the average school. This allows them to focus their attention on the next level of school problems. By using short-term measurable objectives, you and the rest of the educators on your campus will soon be doing the same.

Good luck and great results!

Glossary of Names and Terms

Academically Fragile Student

Any student at risk of academic failure. This can include traditional at-risk factors, such as being economically disadvantaged, or local at-risk factors, such as being a national disaster evacuee.

Accelerated Reader (AR)

A guided reading intervention that involves student reading of selected books, teacher monitoring, and short quizzes. For more information, visit www.renlearn.com/ar.

Advance Placement (AP)

Thirty-seven courses that are aligned with, and prepare a student to take, an Advance Placement exam. Many colleges give students varying levels of additional credit based on AP exam results. For more information, visit www.collegeboard.com/student/testing/ap/about.html.

Advancement via Individual Determination (AVID)

AVID is an elective course that is designed to prepare B, C and D students for the requirements and expectations of a four-year college. AVID classes can be offered in grades four through twelve. For more information, visit www.avidonline.org.

Bloom's Taxonomy

Initially developed in 1956 by a team led by Dr. Benjamin Bloom, the taxonomy divides the cognitive domain into six levels. From lowest to highest, the levels are knowledge, comprehension, application, analysis, synthesis, and evaluation.

Brown, E. Don

Former President of the National Association of Secondary School Principals (NASSP). He is a recognized expert in school improvement and one of the architects of "Breaking Ranks," the NASSP model for secondary school reform. For more information, visit www.leadyourschool.com.

Common Assessment

A performance instrument for a subject that all teachers use and all students take. For example, an Algebra 1 common assessment would be administered to all Algebra 1 students on the campus. Common assessments are generally used to gather instructional data.

Cornel Notes Process

A structured and specific way to take class notes designed to facilitate retention and test taking performance. For more information, web search "Cornell Notes."

Daggett, Willard

Founder of the International Center for Leadership in Education (ICLE), based in New York. He is the creator of the Application Model, a practical planning and instructional tool for determining the relevance of curriculum and assessment to real-world situations. The Application Model is part of the Rigor/Relevance Framework, which has become a cornerstone for a number of school reform efforts. For more information, visit www.leadered.com.

Discipline Continuum

This involves the procedures and practices that dictate specific student consequences for inappropriate student behaviors and actions. Effective discipline continuums are designed to provide the minimum level of consequence to effect a positive change in behavior.

Dual-credit Course

This is a course taken by a student in which he or she can earn both high school and college credit. Dual-credit courses are generally taken either at the high school, college, or on-line. For more information, contact your state education agency and/or local colleges.

Hyper-monitoring

The practice of professional support staff conducting 20 to 25 classroom observations each week, using a common walk-thru protocol, such as PowerWalks. The purpose of this practice is to provide the entire campus with objective data on the current quality of instruction. The author is a pioneer of this concept. For more information visit the Lead Your School website at www.leadyourschool.com.

International Center for Leadership in Education (ICLE)

A school improvement organization that is based in New York, but works nation-wide. ICLE provides speakers, consultants, and support for client districts and campuses engaged in improvement initiatives. For more information, visit www.leadered.com.

Laird, Michael

Assistant Superintendent in Splendora Independent School District. While principal, Dr. Laird's campus experienced dramatic improvements in student performance. To date, he is experiencing similar success in his new role. For more information, visit www.splendoraisd.org.

Leading Indicator

A result that generally suggests the expected nature of another result. For example, six weeks grades should be an indicator of the expected grade on a final.

Lexile Score

A reading instrument that measures both reader ability and text difficulty on the same scale. Lexile scores are often considered more accurate than measures based on grade level. For more information, visit www.lexile.com.

Marzano, Robert

Dr. Marzano is an education researcher, speaker, and author of numerous texts. He specializes in translating research into practical suggestions and actions for practitioners. For more information, visit www.marzanoandassociates.com.

National Association of Secondary School Principals (NASSP)

Professional organization for current and former middle and high school administrators. For more information, visit www.nassp.org.

Objective, long-term

For the purposes of this book, an objective in which the targeted result is measured in a time frame of one year, or longer.

Objective, short-term

For the purposes of this book, an objective in which the targeted result is generally measured in a time frame of one semester, or less.

Price, Thomas

Superintendent of Splendora Independent School District in Texas. To date, Dr. Price has led two school districts in dramatic improvements in student performance. For more information, visit www.splendoraisd.org.

Process

A means to the end. For example, teacher literacy training is a process that should lead to improved student reading performance. Processes are important if they produce the desired results.

Results

What actually occurred. Results are the score, the grade, the attendance percentage, the number of office referrals, etc.

Rigor / Relevance Framework

A tool created by Dr. Willard Dagget for the development of quality lessons. The framework allows the user to assess the quality of a lesson based on the dimensions of knowledge and application. For more information, visit www.leadered.com.

Schlechty, Phillip

Dr. Schlechty is a nationally recognized author and speaker on the topic of school reform. He is the founder and CEO of the Schlechty Center for Leadership in School

Reform, based in Kentucky. For more information, visit www.schlechtycenter.org.

Schmoker, Mike

Dr. Schmoker is an education researcher, speaker, consultant, and writer. He argues convincingly for the need of schools to change their practices dramatically, now. For more information, visit www.mikeschmoker.com.

Socratic Questioning

One of the oldest strategies for provoking critical thinking by students. It is a teaching technique in which the original question is treated as it were the answer. This leads to deeper discussions and better understanding as the discourse continues. Some simple examples of Socratic Questions are, "What is a measureable objective," and "Why is a measurable objective important?" For more information, web search "Socratic questioning."

Telephone Game

A game played by a group of people. The participants stand in a straight line. A message is whispered to the first person in line. This person then whispers the message to the next person, who then does the same to the next person, all the way down the line. The last person then repeats the message that he or she heard to the whole group. The original message and the last message are generally quite different.

Works Cited

Allington, R. (2002). What I've learned about effective reading instruction. *Phi Delta Kappan, 83*(10), 740–747.

Biancarosa, C., & Snow, C. E. (2006). *Reading next – A vision for action and research in middle and high school literacy: A report to Carnegie Corporation of New York* (2nd ed.). Washington, DC: Alliance for Excellent Education.

Carr, C.G. (1994). The effect of middle school foreign language study on verbal achievement as measured by three subtests of the Comprehensive Tests of Basic Skills [Abstract]. *Dissertation Abstracts International – A 55*(07), 1856.

Geiser, S. (2008). Back to the basics: In defense of achievement (and achievement tests) in college admissions. *CSHE: Research and Occasional Paper Series*, 1–8.

Lazear, D. (1998). *The rubrics way: Using MI to assess understanding.* Tucson, AZ.: Zephyr Press.

Human Resources and Skills Development Canada (2000). *Dropping out of high school: Definitions and costs.* Retrieved Feb. 11, 2009, from http://www.hrsdc.gc.ca/eng/cs/sp/hrsd/prc/publications/research/2000-000063/page01.shtml

Marzano, R., Pickering, D., & Pollock, J. (2004). *Classroom instruction that works: Research-based strategies for increasing student achievement.* Alexandria, VA.: ASCD.

McClure, J. E., & Spector, L. C. (2003). Behavior and performance in the economics classroom. *Educational Research Quarterly, 27*(1), 15–23.

O'Brien, E., & Rollefson, M. (June 1995). Extracurricular participation and student engagement. *NCES Education Policy Issues,* 1–2.

Olson, L. (2000, March 29). Study links dropout rate with course requirement. *Education Week, (19)*29, 6.

Parker, C. E., Louie, J., & O'Dwyer, L. (2009). New measures of English language proficiency and their relationship to performance on large scale content assessments. *Issues and Answers Report, REL*(066), 1–60.

Rowan-Kenyon, H. T., Bell, A. D., & Perna, L. W. (2008). Contextual influences on parental involvement in college going: Variations by socioeconomic class. *Journal of Higher Education, 79*(5), 564–586.

Schlechty, P. C. (2005). *Creating great schools: Six critical systems at the heart of educational innovation.* San Francisco, CA.: Jossey-Bass.

Schmoker, M. (2006). *Results now: How we can achieve unprecedented improvements in teaching and learning.* Alexandria, VA.: ASCD.

Wright, B. D., & Stenner, A. J. (1999). Lexile perspectives. *Popular Measurement, 2*(1), 39–40.

Made in the USA
Lexington, KY
03 August 2016